How to Invest

Your Way to

Wealth

- Second Edition -

Nov 2000

How to Invest

Your Way to

Wealth

- Second Edition -

Charles E. Mellon

Published in the United States by:

Sierra Newport Publishing, Inc.
5015 West Sahara #125
Las Vegas, NV 89102

Printed in the U.S.A.

Copyright © 1996, 1999

by Charles E. Mellon

Library of Congress No. 97-091587

ISBN # 0-9656479-0-0

"This publication is designed to provide accurate and authoritative information in regards to the subject matter covered. It is sold with the understanding that the publisher is not engaged in rendering legal, accounting, or other professional service. If legal or expert assistance is required, the services of a competent professional person should be sought."
From the declaration principles jointly adopted by a committee of the American Bar Association and committee of the Publishers association.

Published in the United States by:
Sierra Newport Publishing, Inc.
5015 West Sahara #125
Las Vegas, Nevada 89102

Table of Contents

Preface

This book is the result of over 25 years of investment experience. Much time, effort and research have resulted in what I hope will be a truly useful guide to assist you in maximizing your investment potential and overall portfolio returns. I have attempted to make this book fun, interesting and useful so that you will consider referring back to it, as needed, over time. Every so often a person gets an opportunity like this to help others with advice and counsel that can unlock new doors of understanding. It is my intent to attempt to do so with this work. By utilizing the methods discussed herein and adhering to the basic strategies you should dramatically increase your chances for future investment success. As you read this book, try to visualize the concepts being discussed and how you can utilize them to improve your investment returns and your overall financial position. Good luck investing!

Basic Foundations

The first few chapters of this book have been designed to give you a basic understanding of the securities markets in the United States. Fundamental terms and discussions of risk have been included in the early chapters to assist you in building a foundation for more esoteric discussions of strategy and technique found later in the book.

Managing Your Portfolio for Maximum Returns

Everyone seeks to make the most from his/her investment dollars. Not all of us do, though, because we often tend to disregard basic investment philosophy as we are caught up in the fervor of stock market investing. Most of us KNOW WHAT TO DO to generate decent investment returns; we just do not always DO WHAT WE KNOW. We violate basic tenets of investing and disregard some of the cardinal rules of successful investment philosophy. In this book we will learn the basic strategies of investing for profit and the short-term and long-term techniques to assure the bulk of our portfolio remains intact during market setbacks, which will inevitably occur from time to time.

Let's begin by describing the two basic types of investing and categorizing them for future reference in this book. The first type of investment strategy we will look at deals with our longer term strategies for growth. It is a "Buy and Hold" strategy that allows us to invest in companies with a long history of strong earnings, usually paying dividends, that dominate their product or industry. Hence, we will call this strategy Buy & Hold. The second primary strategy in the broad category of investing deals with short-term investing; perhaps as short as one to two days, or as long as three months, or so. This is a very short term focus on investments, though, and can be rather high maintenance in actual practice. It is not a strategy where you can "bury your head in the sand" and not be cognizant of daily movements of the marketplace. This strategy we will refer to as the "Momentum Strategy" of investing.

Before beginning to use any one particular strategy or technique, it is important that the reader first determine what mix his portfolio will have. That is, how much of the portfolio will be allocated to longer-term investments and how much to short-term, momentum investing. The usual way most people determine this allocation is by assessing how much risk they are willing to take and how much "action" they require to satisfy their needs for excitement. It can certainly be foolish to use this as an investment criteria, though, because it is really a gambling desire that the investor is looking to satisfy (if he thinks about this strategy first), rather than others which are far more important.

The first one that comes to mind is, naturally, the investor's age. No matter how old a particular investor is, there is a limit on the amount of time one has to earn productive income in our society. As a person gets older, the investor has less and less productive time in which to continue to earn a significant amount of income to be used for investment capital. The investor must, therefore; be more conservative as he/she grows older because there may not be enough time to replace savings that are lost needlessly to unnecessary risks. The first criteria, then, should be age.

The second criteria, of course, involves the amount of money available for investment. If a 50 year old investor has but $10,000 to invest, a long-term, buy and hold strategy is probably not going to provide the necessary capital growth needed for retirement purposes. A percentage adjustment between momentum and buy and hold strategies would, therefore, be required. Although there are no set recommended standards for age versus investment capital, the <u>Table of Compounding</u> illustrated in the next section will show how much money can be generated over time given a particular annual rate of return from investments. This becomes a useful planning tool to assist in determining allocation percentages, as well.

With age and investment amount already determined, I use the following chart as a guideline for percentage allocation. These guidelines refer only to that percentage of the portfolio that is dedicated to stocks, however. If, let's say, half of one's portfolio is to be invested in stocks and the investor is 55 years old, of that portion to be invested in stocks, 25% would be allocated to momentum stocks, and 75% would be of the buy and hold category (as in the chart below).

I recommend the following formula (although it is not a hard and fast rule) for most people who have no prior concepts of fundamental investment allocation.

Investment Allocation by Age

Below age 25	90% Momentum	10% Buy & Hold
Age 25 to 35	75% Momentum	25% Buy & Hold
Age 35 to 50	50% Momentum	50% Buy & Hold
Age 50 to 65	25% Momentum	75% Buy & Hold
Age 65+	10% Momentum	90% Buy & Hold

(There are one or two caveats to the above table involving an overlap some of the age groups. In the event of an overlapping age period, one should use the more conservative formula for a person conservative by nature or where the person may be subject to early retirement or layoff in the ensuing years. Further, the ages 55 and older assume that the investor is currently working and will not be subject to income interruption or early retirement.)

Using the above tables, we should find our optimum portfolio mix and write it down for future reference. In later portions of this book we will be able to readily begin building a portfolio for ourselves by using this percentage factor. Although these tables are only suggested guidelines, using them can help prevent unnecessary hardship in the case of falling investment prices over time.

Looking at the chart on Investment Allocation by Age, we can see that the two categories (Momentum and Buy & Hold) indicate what percentage of our portfolio should be allocated to each category. Momentum stocks can be both high-quality or second/third "tier" stocks. (Stocks that are thought to be potential "high-flyers" because of some current economic or technological advantage that one particular company may have over another company, industry or sector of the market). Many smaller companies with excellent products and bright futures are still considered to be second or third tier. It basically means that they are small in terms of market capitalization (the market value of all outstanding stock). It has very little to do with the quality of a company's product or potential for future profits. Nearly all companies start in this category before their sales reach the billion dollar level, or more.

Buy & Hold stocks will invariably be high quality, industry dominant in nature. Most will pay some dividends. These stocks are also usually referred to as "blue chip" stocks.

Becoming Wealthy

There have been hundreds, perhaps, thousands of books written on the subject of becoming wealthy. All have good ideas for the reader to ponder as he makes up his mind which step to begin first. The secret to wealth for the average person, if there is one, is a fairly simple standard taught in colleges and universities throughout the country. Spend less than you earn and invest the rest. Not that difficult a concept. Yet, many of us seem not to understand the meaning of this phrase.

A person trades his productive daily hours for wages. They may be in the form of hourly pay or a set salary, but a person, nonetheless, trades what time he has during the day for a monetary repayment. Being able to discern what one will make for a day's wages, it is now incumbent upon the wage earner to spend less than what he earned after taxes. Making the proper allocations for savings, educational requirements, insurance costs, housing etc., it now comes time to make an allocation to investing for the future. By spending less than one earns and living modestly, it is quite possible for the average person to retire before the age of 65 with considerable assets, if that is one's goal. I know of many people who have been in modest jobs for many years who have achieved a fair degree of wealth by investing their excess assets in quality stocks over the long-term.

I could name several people I know personally that have built huge (seven figure) assets from modest monthly and annual investments over time. Whether it be in real estate, art, stocks or rare coins, a continued investment program is requisite to long-term financial independence.

I'm not sure why there seems to be a few segments of our society who think tomorrow will never come, but some certainly act as if that were true. How else could one explain the extravagant spending being done by many people in our society today? Huge homes, with huge mortgages, garages full of expensive foreign cars, men and women wearing expensive Swiss watches and Country Club affiliations that cost thousands of dollars annually, are just some of the conspicuous spending habits practiced by a few members of our culture. Nowhere else in the free world does one find this sort of excessive spending except in our society: a society that has the lowest savings rate as a percentage of income in the developed world. It seems as though the prevailing thought is that, "I want all mine now, not later." Well, if that is indeed the case, there will be precious little left for the future. One cannot spend all of what is earned now, perhaps even more, and expect there to be adequate means for tomorrow. Large credit card and consumer debt usurp our individual ability to save and invest. This is an absolute recipe for disaster.

Control spending! Save! Invest well! Make a plan! We must be determined and strong in our resolve to continue investing even when we don't want to. We must be temperate in behavior and consumption. We must be modestly self-assured that through our efforts we will be successful. We must be careful to take calculated risk and not unnecessary risk. We must never invest the "rent money" or what we cannot afford to lose.

These principles haven't really changed since the beginning of time. It helps, though, for each generation to develop its own recognition of these principles as if they belonged singularly to that generation. If we continue as a society to spend far more than we earn, borrowing heavily to finance all our whims and slightest desires, we will eventually see the pendulum swing in the other direction that will make the Great Depression seem like just a minor setback in comparison.

When I speak to young investors and students, I remind them of something that perhaps our generation has forgotten. It is the power of compounding. Investing a small amount of money on a consistent basis over time can generate a huge amount of capital in 20 to 30 years. That may sound like a long time, but if we are lucky, that day will eventually come and we'll be around to reap the profits and enjoy the fruits of our investments. Sometimes, I use different examples when I show people compounding tables, but I've chosen one here that I think explains fairly well the dramatic benefits from consistent investment.

The Power of Compounding

15% Annual Return

	1 Year	5 Years	10 Years	20 Years	30 Years
$50 Month	$651	$4,484	$13,933	$75,798	$350,491
$75 Month	$977	$6,726	$20,899	$113,697	$525,737
$100 Month	$1,302	$8,968	$27,866	$151,596	$700,982
$150 Month	$1,953	$13,452	$41,799	$227,393	$1,051,473
$200 Month	$2,604	$17,936	$55,731	$303,191	$1,401,964
$250 Month	$3,255	$22,420	$69,664	$378,989	$1,752,455
$300 Month	$3,906	$26,904	$83,597	$454,787	$2,102,946

20% Annual Return

	1 Year	5 Years	10 Years	20 Years	30 Years
$50 Month	$669	$5,173	$19,118	$158,074	$1,168,040
$75 Month	$1,004	$7,759	$28,667	$273,112	$1,752,060
$100 Month	$1,228	$10,345	$38,236	$316,148	$2,336,080
$150 Month	$2,007	$15,518	$57,355	$474,222	$3,504,120
$200 Month	$2,677	$20,691	$76,473	$632,296	$4,672,160
$250 Month	$3,346	$25,864	$95,591	$790,370	$5,840,200
$300 Month	$4,015	$31,036	$114,709	$948,444	$7,008,241

Mutual Fund Investing

Many people, if not most, feel that mutual fund investing is the way to play the stock market with limited risk. They feel that with the professional management and diversification that is an inherent part of each fund that they can relax and feel comfortable knowing that professionals will achieve a return for them that is probably as good as what the market will provide in any type of investment vehicle.

This is not necessarily true, however. Mutual funds are an excellent vehicle for the small investor who wants some exposure to stocks to provide for long-term growth, and mutual funds certainly do diversify their investments because of their nature and size. The cost of professional management and fund diversification is not always recognized by fund investors, though. The cost is usually manifested in lower returns than what could be achieved by the individual investor himself. Each mutual fund has administrative expenses, commission costs and management fees, etc. Many of these costs vary greatly from fund to fund.

Performance will also vary from fund to fund, and from fund family to fund family. What is important for the investor to know is that the funds' prospectus spells out in detail, exactly what the fees and expected expenses are for the fund in any given period. Each fund is required, annually, to make earnings, net asset and performance reports available to existing investors (with quarterly updates) and to provide interested potential investors with similar information, as well. This is important information that the investor should read carefully before deciding to invest. A mutual funds' overall return last year is certainly no indication of what it will be in the future. Many times as a particular fund gets larger in size, performance declines dramatically. Also, mutual fund investment returns don't generally begin to approach what an investor can achieve on his own with just a little bit of research and guidance.

Mutual funds can rarely outperform disciplined individuals who adhere to proven methods and are willing to do their own investigation and research.

A mutual fund with an annual return to investors of 20% is quite good. An annual return of 20% to an informed individual investor who makes his own decisions is not, however. Funds do, though, have a place in the portfolio of many people. An Individual Retirement Account, for example, is a good place for investing in mutual funds. With an annual commitment of only $2,000, it would be hard for an individual to get the same diversification in any other vehicle. Also, with such a small amount contributed but once a year, commission expenses could be prohibitive. A mutual fund, therefore, probably makes sense in this type of situation.

Careful scrutiny is required, though, to make sure that the funds' performance and investment objectives are commensurate with that of the investor. Many funds are burdened with risky investments in very volatile stocks in an effort to improve the performance of the overall fund. An investor must be very aware of how a fund manager views these types of investments and what actions would be taken to protect investors, from a fund manager's standpoint, should the market take a quick reversal.

When in doubt, talk to the funds' representative. Each fund has an investor relations department (and, usually, regional representatives) that are prepared to answer questions of this sort from investors. The funds' investor relations department, will be able to answer all the questions regarding the funds' performance and investment objectives. A conversation with them may very well soothe whatever reservations or concerns the investor may have about the fund. There are rating services available, too, which an investor can rely on to help him make his investment decisions. Morningstar is one such rating service that specializes in mutual funds. It is, perhaps, the most comprehensive of mutual fund rating services and can give several unique details about a funds performance versus its' investment risk, overall fund volatility, and many other important factors that a potential investor would definitely want to know. Morningstar Reports are available at your local library and from your stockbroker. Proper use of this type of information can, and will, save you from making uninformed decisions that can hurt long-term investment performance.

In determining what to look for in mutual fund investing and how to gauge a fund properly, I use some of the following criteria that will give a good picture of a fund and allow for comparison of one fund to another.

The first thing that I look for in a fund is, obviously, total return. I mean, how much money would I have made if I had bought this fund on January 1st of this year. I want to know in percentage terms, too, what the funds' overall performance was so that I can compare it to other funds. I like to see the 1, 3, 5 and 10 year total returns to get an idea of how consistent the fund managers' performance and judgment has been over the years. It's an excellent tool for comparing one fund to another. Beware of the fund that has had a huge gain in the last 12 months, yet poor returns in the last 3-5 years. Anyone can get lucky in the market but that doesn't necessarily mean that we would want to invest with them.

The second thing that I look for is the investment objective of the fund. Does it look for dividend paying stocks to hold for long term gains, or is it more of a short term trading fund comprised of high risk technology sector stocks and bio-technology companies? I want the fund to have the same objective that I do in my own purchases.

Thirdly, an examination of the Beta of the fund would be appropriate. Beta is the relative volatility of the fund when compared to the market as a whole. A Beta of 1.0 would mean that the fund is equivalent in volatility to the overall market. A Beta of less than 1.0, let's say, .75 would indicate the fund is 25% less volatile than the overall market. Conversely, a Beta of more than 1.0 means the fund is more volatile.

Further, I would look for a breakdown of the funds major portfolio holdings. These are listed in the Morningstar Report and in the prospectus that the fund is required to give the investor before buying. I like to look for company names that I'm familiar with so that I can have confidence in the management of the fund. (If the fund management likes many of the same stocks that I do, I feel good.) Following that, I look for several things in various order (all of which are particularly important, but can be weighted in a similar light):

fees (annual management fees; commission charges for purchase of the funds' shares, etc.); portfolio turnover; rating of the fund by Morningstar (mainly for safety); and average dividend income to the fund as an annual percentage. I look at the total dividend income as a percentage of overall fund growth to determine what the net performance is. If a fund is up 10% for the year and 3% of that gain was in dividend income, I probably would decide not to invest. Why pay a management fee, for a net return of only 7%, to a fund that collects dividends and provides only mediocre investment performance?

With this information, I am now fairly well armed and informed so that I feel confident comparing the opportunities of one fund versus another. When in doubt, though, it's comforting to know that one can rely on Morningstar's rating. After all, they are professionals at the rating game and do an excellent job in providing potential investors with timely, accurate information.

An investor should also be aware of back-end loaded (12B-1) funds. These funds are sometimes sold on the basis of being commission free if the owner holds them through the penalty period (usually 5 years). That's not completely accurate. The fund actually borrows the money to pay the commission to the selling broker. The interest cost of borrowing usually results in lower comparative yields than that of other non-12B-1 funds. Furthermore, many 12B-1 funds have higher management fees than front-loaded funds. These fees all come out of performance (portfolio) income. It is necessary to read the prospectus to determine all the fees that are to be paid from income so that the investor will know what to expect. All funds are not created equal and many funds have high fees that can also subject holders to high penalties for early withdrawal. Being subjected to rear-end penalties is especially disturbing when the fund has declined in price due to poor investment performance. In this case, it is entirely possible that an investor could actually get back less money than originally invested, even after several years investment in the fund.

U. S. Treasury Securities

There is no real secret to investing in U. S. Treasury obligations that we will learn in this chapter, but there are some derivative securities on U. S. Treasuries that are quite useful in assisting the investor in planning for long term situations and consequences. Let's take a look at some facts about Treasury Bonds and how they can be used to benefit the average investor.

U. S. Treasury bonds ("T"-Bonds) are issued in minimum denominations of $5,000 and have maturities from 10+ years to 30 years (the 30-year-bond is what is referred to as the "long bond" on the nightly newscast). The bonds carry an interest rate which is paid semi-annually to bondholders. The bonds are registered in the name of the owner and can be purchased directly from the Federal Reserve through a Federal District Bank, or from any commercial bank or securities brokerage company.

Several years ago, a few enterprising brokerage firms decided to begin trading in a derivative form of this Treasury security. It would pay no interest but could be purchased at a deep discount to face value (maturity value). These new securities were coined "Strips". It meant that they were stripped of all interest payments, but would become worth their maturity value on the maturity date many years hence. These securities are now also referred to in the industry as "Zero Coupon Bonds" because they, obviously, pay zero interest. The strips represent ownership of an actual bond which is held in trust by the financial institution or brokerage firm. Many of these strips can sell for only $600 to $700, but would be worth $10,000 at maturity in 25 to 30 years, or so. It gives many people an opportunity to buy a direct obligation of the U.S. Government that never before could afford to do so. It represents the ultimate safety in investments, too. An obligation that the U.S. Government must pay; backed by its full-faith, credit and taxing authority.

The big advantages to these securities were not only that they became affordable to the masses, but that they could be purchased in nearly any denomination. These securities can be purchased in denominations of only $1,000 rather than the $5,000 minimum on regular Treasury Bonds. So, an investor with an Individual Retirement Account who contributes $2,000 annually might be able to buy $10,000, $15,000 or $20,000 worth of bonds each year (due in 30 years) with his small contribution. It provides an excellent planning tool for educational purposes and for retirement. Imagine the peace of mind for investors in knowing that in 30 years they will definitely have $15,000 or $20,000 coming due each and every year from Uncle Sam. (This can be a big boost to overall retirement income, for sure). It can help balance a portfolio, in terms of risk, over the long haul, too. It can, and does, assist pension plan managers in providing for retirement and medical benefits to participants.

These securities can also make great gifts for grandchildren for educational purposes. Just a few hundred dollars can help provide grandparents significant benefits for their grandchildren for college or private schooling. These zeros can be purchased for shorter term periods, too. A 12, 13 or 14 year, or even 16 year bond may be purchased.

So, these securities can certainly be quite useful for future event planning purposes (education, retirement, etc.) Also, I've heard of these securities being used for promotional purposes by businesses. One such story involves an automobile dealer who gave away a $5,000 bond with the purchase of each new car. They also work well as incentives for employees who have provided outstanding service for their employers. For only a few hundred dollars an employer could give $5,000 bonuses to key employees and dispense significant loyalty and goodwill in the process.

There is a drawback to these investments, though. It is something called "Phantom income". It represents what the IRS says is taxable income, although the investor really receives no money. The IRS claims that even though an investor receives no interest payments, the bonds are one year (each year) closer to maturity, and theoretically, worth that much more than what the investor paid for them (this is certainly not the case in real life, though). The IRS says that investors must amortize the amount of the bond, in excess of what they paid for it, equally over the life of the bond and pay taxes on that amount of money. So, let's say for example we had purchased a $10,000 bond for $1,000 due in 30 years. The IRS says that we must pay taxes on a portion of that $9,000 each year for 30 years ($9,000 divided by 30 years = $300 per year). The good news is that when the bond matures in 30 years, there's no tax due on it. That $10,000 will be ours "tax free" to do whatever we want with it. For this main reason, most people look to purchase zeros in their IRA accounts, where the bonds can mature without tax liability and the money is taxed at the regular tax rate only as it is withdrawn from the account after retirement.

These securities are also marketed under different names by different brokerage firms and may be referred to as CATS, Certificate of Accrual--Treasury Securities; or TIGR's, Treasury Investment Guaranteed Receipts. Whatever they are called, they refer to zero coupon bonds on U.S. Treasury Securities. (There are zero coupon bonds on other types of securities and issued by other borrowers. Also, there are some corporate zero coupon bonds in existence and municipal tax-free zero's, too. Caution is advised here when the investor selects which securities he may be purchasing.)

Effective Use of Margin

Nearly every portfolio manager I know, except those managing mutual funds, uses some degree of leverage to magnify profit potential. The effective use of margin is extremely important in wealth building for the individual because it gives the investor so much more buying power for every dollar of cash available for investment. Margin borrowing, by definition, is the purchase of securities with cash and borrowed funds. The securities themselves act as collateral for the loan which is then repaid when the securities are sold (hopefully at a profit). For decades now, the maximum buying power that this type of leverage produces is 200% of the cash amount available to invest. If an investor had, say $10,000, he could borrow another $10,000 to give himself a total "Buying Power" of $20,000. If he were to purchase $20,000 worth of stocks, his equity would be 50% of the total and his "Margin Debit" (the amount owed) would also be 50%. When the margin requirements were last changed many years ago, (they're set and controlled by the Federal Reserve

Board), the maximum margin amount was established at 50%, which is where it remains today.

I believe that using borrowed money in this fashion is prudent. It is really up to the investor to help control the risks involved in margining his transactions by <u>not</u> borrowing to the maximum extent possible. As mentioned previously, the Federal Reserve Board allows up to 50% of a stock purchase (on most stocks) to be used with borrowed funds, but I feel that amount too risky for many investors. I usually counsel people to not use more than 25% in borrowed money when purchasing on margin. This gives the investor that "added boost" to portfolio profits, but keeps him out of trouble should the overall market, or his particular stock, decline dramatically. After all, the borrowed money will have to be repaid, and if the investor has no additional cash with which to meet a "margin call," his securities will be sold immediately at the current market value (which will always be less than what was initially paid for the stock). So careful use of margin is recommended.

Margin, by itself, is a very useful tool if used diligently. We must not be afraid to use it to our advantage. Think of the many times that we have had profitable trades that could have been enhanced by 25% or more using margin. If we do our "homework" on stock selection, margin can be an important ally in providing superior investments results. We should always consult with our financial advisor, though, to make certain that margin fits with our overall investment objective and our tolerance for risk.

Risk

What do we mean when we talk about risk tolerance in relationship to our investments? Well, no one really likes to take a lot of risk with their investments. Oh, don't get me wrong, we're all willing to take the high returns; we just don't want to take any undue risk to achieve them. So how, then, do we go about determining what the proper risk level is, and what investments may be appropriate given that risk level?

Well, it's easier than imaged, at first blush, to determine what the risk level should be. It is a lot more difficult to determine what our risk level actually is. Each of us is unique in our own way and has pre-conceived notions about risk and risk tolerance. I could dedicate this entire book to risk tolerance but it wouldn't change anyone's mind as to what their tolerance should be. We all have our own ideas as to what risk is and nothing that anyone else says to us is going to make us change our minds. Basically, that's because we are investing OUR money, not someone else's, and no one is coming to our rescue should we lose money in the process of listening to someone else's advice. So, let's take a look at risk as a manageable factor and see how we can identify our risk tolerance and use it effectively to our advantage.

Determining Risk Tolerance

To make a determination of our tolerance for risk we should probably use a phrase of reference that most people would be familiar with. A lot of people would judge their tolerance for an investment by "how well they slept at night". This is probably a good reference to use because we can all relate to sleepless nights where we lie wide awake second-guessing a decision that we made and trying to figure out, "How in the heck could I have been so stupid as to do that?" So, let's use a live example to illustrate that point. Suppose that we had worked hard for nearly 20 years and that we were now nearing 40 years old. We had a family to support, a mortgage payment, car payment, Mastercard and Visa payments and other necessary expenses related to our children nearing college age. Suppose, further, that we had been able to save (with the help of our spouse) nearly $10,000 in cash assets that were not allocated to pending educational needs, medical or dental expenses, vacations or other various and sundry household related expenses every family has. It was $10,000 that was "extra". We didn't want to lose it, but if we did, it would not dramatically change our lifestyle or keep us from enjoying the sunsets (knowing that in a few hours we were going to be in bed for another sleepless night worrying about an investment decision that we had made). Now, using this scenario, we try to put ourselves in the position of this person who decides, without the aid of discussion with his spouse, to buy 1,000 shares of a particular $10 stock that a stockbroker had recommended as a fairly good short-term investment play. Now, as soon as we agree to buy the stock, our broker calls us to confirm the purchase and says that "You bought it at $10 on the offer side of the market, as we agreed, and it's still right in that area now, but the last trade was 9 3/4." (Any problems so far? -- No, good, let's continue.)

That night at the dinner table after the children have left to do their homework, we casually mention to our spouse that we had decided to purchase a stock that our broker had recommended as one with good "upside" potential over the very near term and that we had used the entire amount of our joint savings, $10,000, to buy the stock. Our spouse is uncharacteristically silent at this point and continues to move the food around on the dinner plate in front of him/her. Not knowing what to say, our spouse replies only that he/she wished that they could have been part of the decision making process and that they hoped everything would turn out all right. Nothing much was said the rest of the evening and that night everyone went to bed quietly. (OK, how are we doing so far? Any problems with your sleep tonight? -- Good, let's move on.)

The next day we are preoccupied with work at the office but happen to remember the transaction from the day before and we are just wondering how the "market" was doing, so we reach over and turn on the radio and tune in to the local business station that has periodic market report updates. Just as we do, we hear a report that the Federal Reserve Board was considering an increase in the Discount Rate and that the traders on Wall Street were very leery of the potential for rising interest rates and began "lightening up" on their portfolios (in Wall Street jargon that means they are selling probably 25% of what they owned in stocks causing a large drop in the Dow Jones Industrial Average). Not being sure what all this means, we decide to call our broker just to get a "flavor" for where our stock was trading in relation to the overall market. Our broker replied that an increase in the Discount Rate meant higher interest costs for businesses and individuals because banks would probably raise their prime lending rates. He also explained that bond prices would decline to increase yields to investors and that stocks would follow suit. "Fine", we reply. "Just as I thought," we continue. "What is the price of my stock right now, though?", we ask. The broker replies that although the market was down some 60 points, our stock is holding up very well, all things considered. It was currently trading at about $8 1/2 per share and seemed to be stabilizing in price and that we should not worry further.

That night when we get home from work, our spouse casually asks how the stock was doing that we had purchased in the joint account since he/she had heard the market had dropped some 60 points during that day. We reply something about not knowing that he/she had an interest in the markets because the two of us had never even discussed the stock market in nearly 18 years of marriage. That night all was quiet again and everyone went to bed without much further discussion on investments.

(How do we feel now? Do we still feel confident in the decision that we made to buy? -- Good, let's go on.)

As luck would have it, the very next day the Chairman of the Federal Reserve Board announced an increase in the Discount Rate of 1/2%. "Not toooo bad", we thought. "I wonder how it is affecting the stock market?", we ask ourselves. Not being able to contain ourselves any longer, we pick up the phone and call the broker. Our broker said that the market did not react very favorably to the rate increase. He said it had come rather unexpectedly and that the "Street" (meaning Wall Street) had been basically unprepared for a 1/2 point rate increase. Conventional analysis had indicated a 1/4 point increase as the probable maximum. This caused much more selling than was usual for an increase in the Discount Rate. He predicted further bloodletting over the near term but after that the market would probably stabilize. When asked by us about OUR stock he said that it, too, had been subjected to additional selling and that it was OFF about 3/4 of a point ("off" means DOWN in the investment business. They use that word because it sounds better than the word "down"). "Down about 3/4 of a point," we say. "Well, that doesn't sound so bad. What is the price of it if I were to sell it at this level?", we ask. The broker explains that the last trade on the stock was $7 3/4, down 3/4 of a point from yesterday, but if we were to sell the stock, we would get the "bid price" which at the current time was $7 1/4. "Wow", we think, "I've only had this stock for a few days and already I'm losing nearly $3,000". "OK, thanks for the information," we reply to the broker; too stunned to say anything more intelligent to him and too confused to ask further pertinent questions about the market. Unable to concentrate fully on our business, we decide to go home early for the day to spend some "quality time" with our family. As soon as we walk in the front door we realize that our spouse had returned home from work early, as well. Our spouse asks how everything is going at the office since it is the first time in nearly 10 years that we have ever come home this early before. "Is there anything bothering you?", our spouse wants to know. We reply off-handedly that everything is fine and that we just wanted to spend some quality time with the family, having finished up an important project in less time than expected. Everything seems to be going well until the 6:00 news comes on television and the whole family is watching it in the living room. "The Dow Jones Industrial Average closed down 165 points today in very heavy trading," the nightly newscaster says. Quickly, the whole family turns their heads and looks at our reaction knowing that we have recently purchased stock for the benefit of the "entire family" so that Jr. can go to that special college, that we can put in the swimming pool like our neighbors and that maybe our spouse could have that necklace which was wanted so badly. Mustering all our thespian abilities we assure them that we have spoken to our broker today and he said the investments had only been "off" a little (using a word that we had just learned, realizing that they had no idea what it meant). The explanation seemed to go over very well and the rest of the night was quite pleasant. We did feel a little guilty in misleading the family about the stock value, though. "It will probably come right back up tomorrow," we hope. For now, off to bed. (What is our feeling at this point? Can we still sleep all right? Do we still feel confident that we made the right decision even though our timing might not have been perfect? Can we live with the consequences of a "paper loss"? -- OK, good; let's continue.)

"Nothing goes down forever," we say to ourselves driving to work. "I'm going to call my broker as soon as I get to the office and get an early morning update." After stopping at a customer's place of business on the way to work, we arrive near our usual time and trot into the office with a determined and confident air. As soon as our secretary sees us she calls our name. "Urgent" is all that we hear. Something about, "call our broker," she replies to our inquiry. Now, we go directly into our office without stopping for our usual cup of coffee, which the staff has already poured for us; dial the telephone, before even sitting down, and drop our car keys on the desk loudly before nearly knocking over our swivel chair attempting to jump into the seat. Our broker's now on the line and says that the news that everyone has been waiting for was released this morning before the market opened. It seems that the news was not nearly as good as everyone had hoped and that the company's sales for the period had been much lower than expected. Our broker apologized, but suggested that we sell the stock when it opens for trading because the "analysts" had now put out a near-term SELL recommendation on the stock which was surely to affect its future upside potential in a negative way. "What's the current price?", we ask. The broker explains that the stock has been temporarily suspended from trading and when it opens back up he will have a current price at that time. "Wait a minute," our broker insists, "It just opened for trading." Our broker tells us that our stock is now bid at $5.00 per share and volume appears to be very heavy. "Not a good sign," he says. Not being able to make ourselves take a five thousand dollar loss this early in the morning, we instruct our broker to wait until we call him back for further instructions. We have a sinking feeling in the pit of our stomach; we close the door to our office and tell our secretary not to disturb us unless the boss calls. (OK, now. What is the general consensus at this point? Can we still hold up in the face of adversity? Will we "tough it out" and hold no matter what? Can we sleep tonight? -- Good, get ready, it's not over yet.)

That evening our neighbors drop over unexpectedly for a visit after dinner while walking their two dogs in our front lawn. We are cordial (they've been neighbors for more than 10 years) and casually invite them into the house for a chat. We get around to talking about current events and the subject of the stock market comes up. Our neighbor mentions that he heard of a public company that competes with the company he works for that recently came out with earnings that were disastrous. "We're going to put them out of business," he chimes. Suddenly, we realize the name of the company is the same as the stock that we own. We rapidly put two and two together (yes, we do get four) and decide to exploit this conversation with our neighbor to try to find out more about the company. "Poorly run," says our neighbor. "They make a good product, but can't seem to get it to market on time. Really poor management," he says. "Glad I don't own any of THEIR stock," chortles our neighbor "I'd do myself in," he laughs. At this point in the conversation we get up off the couch and say how nice it was of them to stop over and that we wished that they could have stayed longer but we understand how busy they are and would they please come again when they could stay longer. Our spouse thinks that was rather abrupt of us to be so impatient with the neighbors but said nothing further about it until bedtime. "Is there something wrong?" our spouse wonders aloud, "You seem to be on edge lately." "No, just tired," we respond, "I'm going to bed." (Wow, how do we feel now? Can we handle the pressure? Are we able to sleep at night? -- Good, there's more.)

The next morning we call our broker from the office right after the market opens and inquire about our position. The broker mentions the fact that he told us to sell yesterday when the stock was around $5.00. Now, with the bid at 3 7/8 we have a major loss in the stock. We have a "paper loss" (not a real loss unless you sell) of nearly 70% of your investment, including commission charges. "What would you like to do?" our broker inquires. "Nothing. I'll call you," we reply hanging up on him. Wishing we had talked this investment over with our spouse first, (at least WE would have someone to blame) we spend the day trying to figure out how to break the news to the family that the market was to blame for this loss and it was certainly not our fault. After all, who can predict the stock market?

The family was quiet at the dinner table that evening. It seemed that they could all sense that we were about to say something profound to them that might, even change their lives. Unable to muster the courage, though, we say nothing hoping that tomorrow might bring better news. (Can we live with it? -- Good, we are tough. Let's continue.)

The next morning, after the market dropped 250 points the previous four trading days, the market rebounds with the DJIA opening up 50 points. Hearing this on the radio, we immediately dial our broker and ask about our stock. "It's still the same as yesterday," he says. "But how can that be?" we implore. "The market is up 50 points, surely my stock will be up today. Are you sure you're getting accurate quotes on my stock? It must be going up, you have to be mistaken," we plead. Our broker explains that the Dow stocks are higher because of the recent sell-off. It's just a rebound effect and probably won't last. The market has broken its trend line and it will probably continue to decline over the near term. "You should get out now," he explains, "the bid is $3.00, that's the best you're going to do in this market." Not feeling too well now, we thank him for his time and mention that we will probably take his advice, but that we must first discuss it with the family. "I thought you were going to do that a couple of days ago," the broker interns. Feeling helpless and alone, we thank the broker again and hang up. Tonight, we decide, we will definitely tell the family the truth.

Pushing our food around on our dinner plate, we decide that now is the time to tell our family about the predicament that we have gotten them all into. There will be no swimming pool, no special college for Jr., no special presents for our daughter or our spouse. It seems that everything the family held dear would now evaporate into thin air because of our mistakes in judgment and our obstinate holding on to a stock that was sure to go down the drain. "I have an announcement to make," we say, as the family looks up in wonderment, knowing that whatever was on our mind we now feel compelled to share with them. Just at that moment the doorbell rings. Our spouse rises to answer it before we can finish our sentence (and our confession). At the door is our neighbor smiling brightly. Walking into our dining room, he exclaims that our family was now looking at the President of a new division; one that they had just agreed to acquire that day. "Remember that little company that we were talking about the other night. The one that had such poor management and all," he says to us. "Yes, of course I remember," we respond. "Well, my company just agreed to buy it. You'll be hearing the news on TV any minute now. The exchange stopped trading in the shares late this afternoon pending our announcement of the agreed buyout. My company is buying theirs for $18.00 per share. "If you owned the stock you could have made a fortune. It's was trading as low as $3.00 today," our neighbor said. "I do own it, or we do, our family I mean," we reply. "That's the announcement I was just about to make to the family before you came in. We nearly doubled our money in just two weeks," we cackle. "I was just going to tell the whole clan that we're going to put in that swimming pool like you have next door," we continue, feeling overwhelmed with our new good fortune. "Great," replies our neighbor. "I have to be going now, just thought you might like to hear the news," he says as he walks out the front door. The next day we call our broker and sell the stock at $17.50 per share, glad that we were able to get out of a terrible situation in which we were fortunately rescued by fate.

What is our feeling of risk now? How many of us would have sold our stock after the first decline? Would we have been able to sleep at night? Those of us who say that they could have weathered that large drop in price without panic and without loss of sleep have very high levels of risk tolerance and will have no problem making intelligent, unemotional decisions regarding investments. Those of us who had immediate problems with the poor news on the company and the subsequent drop in stock price, have a very low tolerance of risk and should be careful of the types of investments that we make (we'll discuss which one's later) and the amount of money that we invest in the equity side of the markets (stocks). For those of us who felt some discomfort, let's just say that if we were moderately concerned about our situation right up until the end of the above example, that we have a better than average risk tolerance and should do very well investing in the stock market for the long and short term using the guidelines that we will outline in future chapters of this book.

Stocks vs. Bonds

I am a personal believer in the long term benefits of owning stocks over bonds with the exception of the retiree attempting to replace earned income with a constant flow of investment income. If one looks at the total returns for equities (stocks) over nearly any 10 year period of time since the turn of the last century, one finds that equities have dramatically out-performed fixed-income (bonds) securities by a significant margin.

It is for this reason that I usually recommend to my students that they use bonds only as a portfolio hedge when interest rates are high so that they can lock in rates at or near the double-digit level. Otherwise, the equity markets are where most people should be concentrating their investment efforts. Also, there are equity investments, preferred stocks and many utilities, that act like bonds and that pay increasingly higher dividend returns every year (in the case of some utilities). I, therefore, think that unless an investor is preparing for imminent retirement, or his risk tolerance is extremely low, that he should continue to stay in equity type investments to maximize total returns over the longer term.

Diversification and Your Portfolio

Every investor, naturally, wants to make as much money as possible on his investment dollars. Whether it be for purposes of income or growth, all investors want maximum "cash flow" from their portfolios. Sometimes, if this objective is the only one foremost in our minds, it can contaminate our thinking processes by allowing us to completely disregard what our mothers told us about "not putting all our eggs in one basket". In our excitement to get in on a stock before an expected "price soar," we sometimes over-buy the amount of stock that we know is prudent hoping to make a "real killing" and then go back to our more conservative methods the next time. "Just this one time," we say to ourselves, "and never again". "I want to make a big hit and then I'll be more cautious, next time," we promise ourselves. Well, guess what? It seems like every time we do that, it proves to be the wrong time for us. That's why diligent diversification is so much an important part of effective portfolio management that it just, absolutely, cannot be over stated.

Diversification and Your Portfolio

I always suggest, when asked, that investors put no more than 10% of their holdings in any one particular security. That applies, certainly, to portfolios of only average size. The larger the portfolio, the greater the need for additional diversification. Having a $100,000 portfolio may be adequately diversified with 10 separate issues, but a $1,000,000 portfolio would require even further diversification, say up to 15, 20 or more different issues. Although we never like to think that any of our stocks will perform poorly, or that our bonds may be downgraded in rating, history tells us otherwise. Discretion should prevail in all our decisions because our downside is far too great if we don't use good judgment with diversification (just like Mom said). When in doubt, know that it is far better to over-diversify, than to do otherwise.

In the process of diversifying our portfolio, it may be helpful to use the following tables as a guide to a recommended mix of equity (stocks) and debt (bonds) securities. The tables indicate Aggressive growth vs. Conservative growth and are segregated into various age groups. Utilization of these allocation parameters can assist the investor to maintain his asset base during difficult times in the market. It is recommended, though, that a portion of each allocation be set aside in cash for future deployment as investment opportunities arise. (The percentage totals represent the proper allocation for only that portion of the portfolio that is invested at any given time.)

Aggressive

Age 25 to 35 --100% Equity, 0% Bonds
Age 35 to 50 -- 90% Equity, 10% Bonds
Age 50 to 55 -- 75% Equity, 35% Bonds
Age 55 to 65 -- 50% Equity, 50% Bonds
Age 65 +   -- 35% Equity, 65% Bonds

vs.

Conservative

Age 25 to 35 -- 90% Equity, 10% Bonds
Age 35 to 50 -- 75% Equity, 25% Bonds
Age 50 to 55 -- 50% Equity, 50% Bonds
Age 55 to 65 -- 35% Equity, 65% Bonds
Age 65 +   -- 15% Equity, 85% Bonds

Types of Orders

There are a few order-entry strategies that are designed to be employed to greatly assist a portfolio manager in protecting his profits and limiting his losses. One such strategy regards the use of "Stop Loss Orders". Stop loss orders are orders that are placed away from the current market price of a stock and are used for the purpose of protecting the investor from losses if the stock declines, or advances if the investor has "shorted" the stock (hoping that it will go down). They are also very effective, if properly used, to help lock-in profits for those stocks that have increased in price, thereby, protecting the stockholder from profit erosion.

There are two basic types of stop orders, "Sell Loss Stop" orders and "Buy-Stop" orders. We will only be dealing with sell-stop orders in this book because we will only be looking at situations where we are owners of stocks and options which we will be looking to sell for profits or sell to protect from loss. There are also two types of sell-stop orders. A

"Market" order and a "Limit" order. We will only be dealing with sell-stop market orders.

A sell-stop order is placed <u>below</u> the current market price of a stock. It's designed to get us out of a stock when the stock declines to levels that we no longer want to be an owner. In this way, the sell-stop order acts as our ultimate protector (since it is nearly impossible for us to keep watch over our portfolios all day, every trading day); it keeps us from incurring unnecessary losses when we aren't watching the stock. An example of how it can be used effectively is as follows:

Let's say we buy a stock at $15 per share and the stock has climbed to $20 per share. Our first thought might be to "take our profits and run". But, it may also be the worst decision we could make if that stock climbs to $35 or $40 (if we sold it at $20). Yes, we sold at a profit, but look how much money we "left on the table". Having paid $15 for the stock which is now at $20, one could place a stop order at, say, $18 1/2. If the stock declined, the seller would receive less money than if he had sold it at $20, but if the stock continues to rise to $35 or $40, the owner would still have the stock and be participating in the stocks' price increase. (Or course, if the stock declines, the investor has sold his stock for less than current prices, but the transaction is profitable, none the less.) When placing a stop order (a sell-stop), the order becomes a market order when the stock trades at or below the price of the sell-stop. Meaning, that the stock will certainly be sold, but the price may be slightly less than the exact amount of the sell-stop order. This differs from what we referred to earlier as a "Stop-Limit" order. A stop-limit order can only be executed at our limit. So, using the above example, if our stock had declined to $18 1/2 and we had placed a stop-limit order, we may not have sold our stock even if it continued to drop unless we could sell it for, at least, $18 1/2. These types of orders can be dangerous in fast moving markets and that's why I don't like to use them. A stop-order is all I ever use (rather than stop-limit orders), because I know of many situations where great losses have occurred by putting limits on orders that are designed to protect the investor from loss, being rendered virtually useless by poor utilization with stop-limits. One such example happened to a good friend of mine (I wouldn't dare even think of mentioning his name) when he used a stop-limit order to protect him from further losses. He had purchased a stock for $21 per share. The stock was a volatile stock and had been as high as $25 and as low as $5 during the previous several months. The company was well-regarded in its industry, though, and was considered to be capable of going into the $30 range when he bought it. He placed a stop-limit order (obviously without consulting me) at $19 and pretty much forgot about where the stock was trading on a day-to-day basis, feeling quite comfortable with his stop-limit order to "protect" him. The stock dropped dramatically (along with most other technology stocks) one day and traded at 19 1/2, then 19 1/4, and then 18 7/8, before falling to $16 at the close. His order was never executed because he had put a limit of $19 on the sale price. Thinking that he had already sold his stock, though, my friend didn't bother to consult his broker about the status of his order until a couple of days later. By then, the stock was at $11 per share. My friend then calls me and says "What do you think I should do now?". After chastising him for not speaking with me sooner, I told him that if I were him I would sell now and "lick my wounds," because the stock appeared to be headed much lower. He did, and I was right. The stock is now at $5. Had he just used a sell-stop order rather than a stop-limit order, he would have been out of the stock somewhere in the $18+ range. (No further comments would be appropriate here because I know my friend will be reading this book.) Using stop orders effectively will reduce downside damage to a portfolio in a falling market and help maximize profits in a rising one.

Rules of the Game

As I promised, let's discuss ways for staying out of trouble with our investments by laying some ground rules and guidelines for the average investor. One of the most frequently asked questions that I come upon is, "When do I sell to take my profit?". My standard "tongue-in-cheek" answer to that is, "How much money do you want to make?". Really, though, what I'm telling my students is that there is no "pat" answer for how much money we can or should be making with any particular trade. What we like to see is that profitable trades are allowed to run as much as possible and that unprofitable trades are nipped in the bud quickly. Therefore, I've developed some guidelines for successful investing (and these are not just proprietary to me, but common sense and common knowledge, as well) that will help the investor accomplish the desired end.

In dealing with stock investments there are several items to consider. First and foremost is, has the investor done his homework in regard to purchasing the stock. By this I mean, has he done the necessary research on this stock from both a fundamental and technical perspective so that he knows enough about the company to decide whether on not he should own it? Many people just rely on hearsay, or the uninformed opinions of someone else, to determine whether or not to buy. This is pure gambling. An investor must be able to determine what the prospects for a company are before deciding to buy, and in order to determine that, he must know quite a bit about the company. (We'll cover what we need to know at a minimum in future chapters).

After determining when to buy, the investor should, secondly, prepare a defense strategy should the investment not work out the way it's planned. A loss limit needs to be established so that the investor can reduce his exposure to the stock when things just don't work out. And, they don't work out about 30% of the time. After determining the loss limit (I always use 10% of the price of the stock) a sell-stop order should be placed below the current market value, using an "Open" or G.T.C. (good 'til cancel) order, at the same time we have confirmed the purchase of the stock. Limiting the downside of our investments is, at least, as important as maximizing our upside.

Thirdly, a reasonable time-frame should be established in the investors mind as to the length of the investment. If, for example, a stock is purchased with the idea that when earnings are announced next week the stock should move up and then be sold for a profit, that original premise must be kept. In other words, if the earnings are not as good as expected, or if the stock doesn't move up, then the original premise was wrong. The stock did not perform as anticipated, and must, therefore, be sold. Holding on to a stock in hopes of its eventual return to levels of profit has made many a poor person out of a rich one. If our original premise was wrong, everything after that premise is wrong, as well. Admit the miscalculation and move on to other, more profitable opportunities.

If our original premise is correct, and the stock moves up, deciding when to take profits is critical. This is when we use the sell-stop order (discussed in an earlier chapter) to protect our profits, yet let them run as far as possible.

In the case of options investing, it is even more critical to stand by our original premise to protect from loss. Because options move in a magnified nature percentage-wise, an up or down movement in the stock can cause big swings in price movement of options. (Which we love. It's called leverage.) So, in the event an option were purchased with the hope that a particular news item would move the underlying stock up, if that stock doesn't move higher, the options will lose value quickly. I, therefore, set my maximum loss on option purchases at 50% of the price I paid for the option. If I bought the option for $3, I would sell my option for a loss once it dropped to $1 1/2. Conversely, I would look to protect my profits by selling the original dollar amount of my options investment plus a reasonable profit, if the option increases in price, and let the remaining number of options "ride". For example, if I bought 10 option contracts at $3 which are now selling for $5, I would probably sell 8 of the contracts (my original investment plus a reasonable profit) and keep the other 2. This way, if something negative happens to the option price in the future, I have no real investment risk, only an opportunity loss. I would most likely sell the remaining 2 contracts when the option price tripled or when the time remaining before expiration was one week or less.

Market Timing
and Your Investments

It's always interesting to me when I hear people say that they want to invest in a stock just because they heard from a friend that it is supposed to rise 50% to 75% in the next year, or so. I'm thinking, "Well, if that's true, why not just buy it right before it moves, rather than buy it now and hold it for an entire year." The question is, "When is it going to move and how much of that move can I capture on a timely basis?" For the answer to that we have to take a look at some of the technicalities of timing a stocks' movement within the movement of the overall market.

Now, I don't want to get too complicated with this part of our discussion, but it is important that every investor knows when his stock is showing strength and when it is showing weakness. One cannot always tell just by looking at the trading activity alone. To be certain of how our stocks are performing relative to past history, it is necessary to examine a chart on the stocks' activity. Think of a chart as a picture of a stocks' personality. It will show how a stock has reacted in the past, thereby, giving a fair indication of how it may react in the future under similar conditions. Using an analysis of this type of "technical" picture, one can identify certain trends exhibited by stocks that can lead to fairly accurate predications of future trading action. Historically, it has been shown that technical evaluations will be fairly accurate about 70% of the time. That means that using this type of investment "examination" one should be reasonably accurate 7 out of 10 times, which is a pretty good percentage. I use this type of technical evaluation myself, coupled with other evaluation methods, and find it to be accurate 70% to 80% of the time when used in conjunction with strong fundamental factors.

Now, when we look at a stocks' chart, for example, we look for levels of obvious support and resistance. These levels are fairly easy to identify and when identified can represent buying and selling points. When I look at the long term picture of a stock, I look for the levels of support and resistance that tell me if I'm paying too much for a stock or if the stock seems to be forming a basing pattern, at a certain price, in preparation for a large advance, etc. Using the examples below, we can take a look at some classic patterns of stocks that seem to be headed in both directions, (up and down), and what types of patterns to look for and which to avoid.

GOOD PERFORMANCE

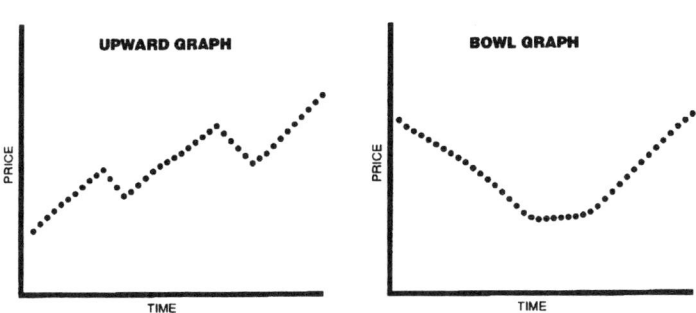

POOR PERFORMANCE

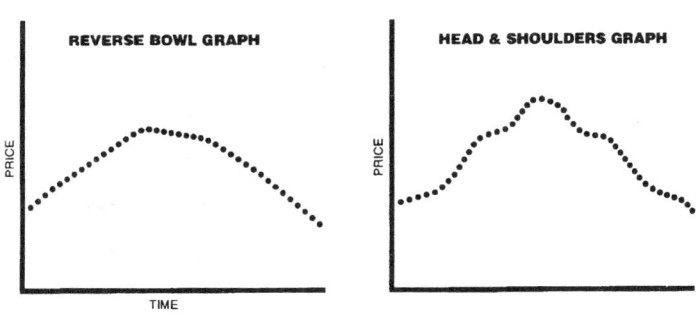

How to Invest Your Way to Wealth

Regarding our opening statement, though, I find it rather strange for someone to want to invest in a stock for an entire year to get a 50% return, when, using some degree of technical analysis, one can get most of that advance, say 75% (of the 50%) in a short period of time, rather than buying and holding for a year. Timing, they say, is everything in life. If that, indeed is the case (and I believe it is), then we should be looking at indicators that help us with our timing as well as with our fundamental investment strategies themselves. Chart reading is one way to be of valuable assistance in that regard.

Most stocks don't (although some do) move in a slightly upwards bias over time to double in price. What usually happens is the stock will move in a level period for some months and then suddenly, over a period of 30 to 60 days move substantially upward before leveling off again. I want to be buying the stock as it moves up, rather than buying and holding for a long period of time. It is true that we will only get 60% to 75% of the move in stock by doing that. But, we will get that move in a very short period of time without having our money tied up unnecessarily. Using this method then, one could play several stocks using the same investment capital over and over again, and get a collective return much greater than if only one stock had been purchased for the long haul. This is the essence of momentum investing. It is the "play of the day" and the "play of the week" that the momentum investor looks for when committing his capital: buying for short periods of time and getting out quickly; maximizing profit potentials to the utmost, while having liquidity to invest in several opportunities in a short time span. This will require diligent effort by the investor to keep in close contact with his investments so that a decision can be made to act quickly, if necessary, not that one would have to be forever linked to a quote terminal, but be available for consultation should a stockbroker call with information favorable to a profitable trade.

Buying Stocks --What to Look For

There are some minimum guidelines that every investor should follow in deciding whether or not, to buy a particular stock. Many of these guidelines are common sense approaches to investing that people may already familiar with. But, most people lose money in the markets because they let emotions get in the way of proper decision-making. Following an established pattern of gathering criteria and careful analysis of data is the way to stay out of trouble in the investment arena.

If we're going to invest in stocks it is always helpful for us to know something about the company that we are planning to invest in. By that, I mean, we should understand what the company does, what product or service it provides to generate revenue, and what the prospects are for future profitable operations. In determining this, I like to look for several specific criteria that will help eliminate those stocks that are not candidates for my portfolio, so that I can concentrate on the ones that are.

Perhaps the first thing that I look at when selecting stocks for investment is sales growth. I want to invest in companies that have an historic track record of increases in sales every year. (I'd like to see sales growth of, at least, 10% year to year.) I'd like to see growth on a calendar quarter basis, as well. I always compare one calendar quarter to the same calendar quarter of the previous year which shows me actual sales growth without seasonal fluctuation.

I want to know what the company does in layman's terms (this is important for investments in computer and bio-technology stocks). What are the specific products or services that the company renders? Who are their customers and clients? How strong is the customer base? Are they in an industry notorious for slow collection of accounts receivable? (For example, any government contractor.) How does the product they provide compare with others available in the industry? Are they leaders in their industry? (Microsoft, Intel, Nike etc.)

If I don't understand what a company does or what product it manufactures, then I can't make an informed decision as to whether or not I want to be an owner. I need to know and understand how this company is going to make me money, and, more importantly, when! I will be unable to determine that, most probably, unless I am thoroughly familiar with what the company does and how it operates.

I want to know about a company's management. Remember when Lee Iacocca took over Chrysler Corp. how the stock jumped? I want my stock to jump, too. I want to invest in companies with strong, experienced management with proven track records of success. (Look at what Lou Gerstner has done for IBM, for example.) Also, there are some Chief Executives that are running companies that I would never invest in only because of them. Some CEOs are so poor at running companies I know it's only a matter of time before the bottom falls out of the stock and I don't want to be left holding the bag. (I have chosen not to use any specific examples of these CEOs for obvious reasons) I like to have faith in the fact that the management is seasoned and capable. The CEO runs the company for the benefit of the stockholders. The stockholders are, after all, the owners of the company.

A strong balance sheet, too, is required to meet continuing challenges of the business environment in this country. I like to take a look at a company's cash-on-hand and their ability to meet current indebtedness. For this reason, I look at some formulas: the current ratio (current assets to current debt) and total-debt-to-equity. (Remember the frenzied merger activity of the 1980's, when the buzz-words were to "maximize shareholder values". This usually meant for the company to go heavily into debt, borrowing money to buy back outstanding shares of stock at inflated prices, and laying off thousands of talented, loyal workers in order to pare expenses to meet the increased costs of servicing the new debt.) I want to avoid companies with heavy debt-to-equity ratios. History tells me that a company can't, and won't, remain competitive in the long run with staggering debt.

Although many high quality companies don't pay dividends, I like to collect dividends whenever possible. I, therefore, look at when a dividend is payable; if I have a choice of two stocks in the same industry group, I try to select the one with the dividend, all other things being equal. I then look at the company's price/earnings ratio. That is the ratio between what each share of stock earns, divided by the current price of that share. (This ratio is also referred to as the stocks' multiple.) At the present time, (October '96) the average stock listed on the NYSE trades at about 19-20 times earnings. The average NASDAQ listed stock trades about 30+ times earnings. (Microsoft trades at about 35 times earnings, for example) I look for stocks that are within these average ranges or less. A high P/E ratio can spell potential trouble for the long-term investor who is unaware of the P/E multiple, although that is not always the case in the high-tech markets.

Finally, I like to see if this is a good time to be investing in the company by viewing the stocks' chart. The technical picture presented by the chart tells me if I am buying at a favorable time (remember, timing is everything in life) for this particular stock. This is not 100% foolproof, but it will definitely be helpful in the decision-making process to evaluate the chart. At this same time, I also like to review any brokerage firm research reports that may be available on the company. I like it when stocks I select have been recommended by major brokerage firms for purchase by their clients. I also like to review the reasons why they think now is a good time to buy. Along with this information, I have the beginnings of a selection process that will help to keep me out of trouble, reasonably maximize my returns and assist me in determining the right time to buy. If the investor uses this method, along with his own, it will only strengthen his ability to maximize potential portfolio returns.

Value Investing

In an earlier chapter, we discussed doing our homework before determining how and when to buy a particular stock. There are other facets to decision-making processes to be considered, as well, that we'll cover to give the reader a well-rounded perspective of the market and stock valuations.

It is fair to say that the markets are, indeed, fickle in nature. If not, how else would we explain that a $40 stock today is more popular than when it was only $30 last week. There seems to be two distinct perceptions within one market that actually influences decisions in our stock market trading strategy. One part involves finding stocks that have real value based on specific standards of accounting principals, for example, and another involves a set of standards that are based solely upon market perception of those values. How the stock might react over the short term to investor perceptions of that stock, and when, is what we want to accurately quantify.

I like to call this, "Perception versus Reality." It is actually just the markets' perception of a stock that induces it to rise or fall. A stock may very well be worth the price it is selling for at the present level, but if investor perception of that stock is substantially different, the stock will likely move up or down, accordingly. It may move up quickly in anticipation of an event that may not happen for years. (This is particularly true in the drug stock sector. An announcement of the discovery of an Aids vaccine, for example, would likely move any stock up 50% or more no matter what the current price.) Or it could fall if earnings per share decline by as little as a penny.

The perception that the market has for value is often tainted, too. Sometimes stock valuations are much too excessive, leaving investors to wonder, "Who's doing all the   buying at these price levels?". Other times, there may be stocks with truly good records of annual earnings increases for many years that are selling incredibly cheap. It is really the markets' perception that an investor wants to gauge and not necessarily the reality of investment value. After all, a stock, just like real estate, is worth only what someone will pay for it.

There have been many instances of undervalued stocks that have been purchased for the long term by investors that have made fortunes. Sir John Templeton and Warren Buffet are perhaps two of the best known value investors, constantly searching for the next opportunity that, as yet, may remain undiscovered by the rest of Wall Street. But, I generally like to look for stocks that are currently in an upswing when buying, stocks whose investor perception is high and getting higher so that I can ride the tide to loftier levels. Much, if not most, stock selection is based on investor perceptions of market value, rather than actual value, which many times is completely irrespective of basic corporate valuation methods. I tend to look for stocks that have shown price improvement and seem to be perceived by investors as good values and ride the "coattails" on the influx of buying. I am a momentum investor at heart and like to take my profits quickly when trends deem to change.

I try not to be tempted with greatly undervalued but unpopular stocks versus those that are undervalued and just becoming popular. I will take the popular stock every time so as to maximize my short-term profit potential. Remember, stocks that are undervalued may be so for a reason, but until the perception on Wall Street changes in regard to that stock, its price will most likely continue to languish.

Options and You

I always get a kick out of people who say that they enjoy investing in stocks but would <u>never</u> touch the options market because it is too risky. The options market <u>is</u> risky, no doubt, but is the stock market not, also? The biggest reason that people lose money in the options market is because they try to use stock strategies for investing in the options market. We can't do that. We have to use options market strategies in the options market in order to be successful. If we attempt to do otherwise, we are only inviting disaster. There are stock options on about 2,000 different companies available for trading. Not all stocks have options, obviously, but there are enough out there available to keep us fully invested if we want to be. Options are derivatives of stocks, and as such, they change price in accordance with the price changes in the underlying stock on which they trade. There are many different types of options: commodity futures options, index options, interest rate futures options; to name a few. We're only interested in stock options in this book, and all of the strategies and techniques we'll discuss relate only to options traded on stocks.

The biggest reason I like the stock options market is because of the leverage it gives. We can "control" a large number of shares of an expensive stock for only a few hundred dollars. The leverage and potential for profit is enormous, so, also, is the potential for loss if we don't know what we are doing. By using the methods we will learn here, we can avoid the painful process of having to "learn by experience". We will already have a strategy for entering and exiting the options market that we will have confidence in using.

Let's start our options discussion by identifying and explaining some terms. First of all, there are two basic types of options. "Calls" and "Puts". (If the investor is not familiar with options trading or these terms, he should call any brokerage office and ask them for the booklet "CHARACTERISTICS AND RISKS OF STANDARDIZED OPTIONS", and they'll be glad to send it. It's published by the stock and options exchanges to benefit and inform potential options clients about the options markets.) Calls are easier for most people to understand than puts are for several reasons as we'll see later. Owning a call basically gives the option buyer the right, but not the obligation, to purchase the underlying stock at a specified price for a certain period of time. As the stock moves up in price, the call option increases in value because the call option owner, has "locked in" the right to buy the stock at a specific price. (Hopefully, that price is less than the stock is currently selling for, but doesn't necessarily have to be for one to make money).

That seems to be easy enough to understand. Puts, though, seem to give everyone problems. A put is an option that gives the owner the right to <u>sell</u> a stock at a certain price for a specific period of time. A put holder (owner) locks in the price at which he would want to be able to sell the stock. Hopefully, that price will ultimately be higher than the stock is currently selling for in the open market. A put holder, therefore; hopes that the price of the stock will go down. As it goes down, his option will be worth more money because he still has a right to sell the stock at a higher price than what the stock is selling for in the open market. (See, that wasn't so bad.) Puts may be a little more difficult to understand, but they can be very profitable investments in a down market. (We can imagine, perhaps, if we owned a put and had the right to sell a stock for $50 per share and the stock suddenly dropped to $35. Our put would be worth a lot of money. We may have only paid a few hundred dollars for the put which would now be worth at least $1,500. (The difference between $50 and $35). In summary, to use an old Wall Street expression, "Buy low; Sell high"; think of puts as a way of being able to sell high when the stock price is low. When we own puts we hope the stock declines. When we own calls we hope that the stock price goes up. It's really that simple.

Option "Contracts" are sold in denominations of 100 shares. Meaning that 1 (one) contract of an option represents 100 shares of stock. Therefore, 10 (ten) contracts would represent 1,000 shares, and so on. Each contract may sell for only $100 or $200, but will represent 100 shares of a stock selling for, perhaps, $50 or $60 per share. So, that for only a few hundred dollars, we can participate in the price movement of a stock worth several thousand dollars just by owning an option on that particular stock.

Options, unlike stocks, have maturity dates, that is, dates when they expire and become worthless. This is what many people feel makes them risky, because if the investor holds options long enough, they eventually will expire and, theoretically, not be worth anything. We do, therefore; have to be nimble when trading options and be aware of how quickly an anticipated move in the stock price will occur. Options trading is not for the "faint at heart," but a great deal of the risk can be eliminated by using the strategies and techniques we will be discussing further in this book.

All stock options expire, technically, on the Saturday following the third Friday of the expiration month. So, if we had a September option, for example, we would know when it would expire by looking at a calendar to see when the third Friday was and the Saturday following it. This seems to be a cumbersome rule to remember, and we really don't care too much when they expire, as much as "When is the last day we can trade them." The last day we can buy or sell them is the last trading day for the option, which is the third Friday. We can say, then, that for our intents and purposes, options expire on the third Friday. If we don't sell them by that time, we're out of luck.

Options are listed on exchanges and are available for us to check on prices daily in the local newspaper, just like stocks. If we follow a particular stock we'll know that it has "Call Letters" or a "Stock Symbol," letters that represent that particular company's stock on its appropriate exchange. (If we don't know the stock symbol we can easily call a local stock brokerage office to find out.) Stocks that are listed on either the New York Stock Exchange or the American Stock Exchange will have one, two or three letters representing that stock. Stocks traded on the NASDAQ exchange or over-the-counter, will have four or more letters that represent the company name. When in doubt, though, just call the stockbroker for assistance. I'm sure he'll be glad to help.

To use an example of stock options, let's check on a fictitious company we'll call XYZ. Both the put and the call on XYZ Company's stock would expire on the same day. It would be listed as an XYZ September _____ put or call. The "_____" in this example is what is referred to as the "Strike price" of the option. It is the price at which we have the right to exercise the option. Strike prices have set, pre-determined increments with the minimum strike price being at $5 per share. For stocks trading less than $25, the strike prices move in increments of $2.50, so there would be a $5 strike price, a $7.50, $10, $12.50, $15, $17.50 and so on, up to $25. From $25 to $200 priced stocks, the strike prices are in increments of $5. ($25, $30, $35, $40, $45 etc.) So, we will always know what strike price to ask for, based on the current price of the stock.

If we wanted to buy a call option on XYZ Company's stock thinking that the stock would increase in value, we would first look to see at what price the stock was trading. Let's say the stock was at $35 per share. We may want to buy an XYZ September $35 call option. That would give us the right, but not the obligation, to buy the stock at $35. If the stock went up to $40, that option would be worth more than we paid for it because we would still have the right to buy it for $35. We would, therefore, just sell that right to someone else in the open market for a profit. We will just sell the option to someone else (and we don't care who) if the stock price goes up. We never buy options to "Exercise" them (to actually purchase the underlying stock); we only buy options to turn around and sell them for a profit if the underlying stock does what we expect it to do. And, because options are listed on an exchange, we don't have to worry about to whom we're going to sell our options. There is a ready and liquid market for our options that is regulated by the exchange the option is listed on, quite similar to stocks.

So, now we know that if we feel a stock is going down, we want to buy a put option on that stock. If a stock we feel is going to up, we would want to buy a call option. Now let's look at some examples that help us decide which options we may want to purchase on a particular stock we feel may go up. In the following example, XYZ company stock has traded at various levels over the near term (between $35 and $47 per share) and is currently at $37. We call our stockbroker and he gives us the prices of some options on that stock at different strike prices which are the following:

September $35 Call ---------- **$ 3 1/2**
September $40 Call ---------- **$ 1 1/2**
September $45 Call ---------- **$ 3/8**

(Remember, each contract is for 100 shares of stock. We must multiply the price of the option by 100. $3 1/2 would really be $350; $1 1/2 would be $150, etc.)

Now, if we wanted to invest in the options thinking that the price of the stock was going to go up we have a choice of scenarios. There is no right or wrong strategy, but some will be more profitable than others. Since we want to make as much profit as possible, let's look at ways to accomplish this using the above prices. If we had a limited amount of money to invest, say around $1,000, we could buy three (3) of the September $35 call option contracts (thereby "controlling" 300 shares of stock), or, we could buy six (6) contracts of the September $40 calls representing 600 shares, or, we could buy about twenty-five (25) of the September $45 contracts, equivalent to 2,500 shares. More is not always better in the options market, but if this stock does what we expect it to let's see how much money we could make on a $1,000 investment.

The stock performs as we had hoped and is now at $39 per share, up $2 from where it was when we bought the options, just two trading days ago. The option prices are now as follows:

September $35 Calls ------------- $ 5
September $40 Calls ------------- $ 2 1/4
September $45 Calls ------------ $ 5/8

The September $35 calls that would have been purchased for $350 each (remember, we could have bought 3 contracts) are now worth $500 each. The September $40 calls that we paid $150.00 each for are now worth $225 each, and the September $45 calls that we paid $37.50 each for are now worth $62.50 each. In terms of percentage movements, the $45 calls made the largest gain, increasing about 66% in value. The $40 calls increased about 50% in value, and the $35 calls were up about 43%. We can see that we get "more bang for the buck," in terms of percentage price movement, in the option that is above the current price of the stock (also called "Out-of-the-money" options) rather than those that are at or near the price of the stock. This will nearly always be true with very few exceptions. Our three scenarios then, representing a $1,000 investment in each option would have provided the following total returns (excluding commission charges).

Scenario A
September $35
3 contracts = $1,050
Sold @ $5 = $1,500

Scenario B
September $40
6 contracts = $900
Sold @ $2 1/4 = $1,350

Scenario C
September $45
25 contracts = $938
Sold @ $62.50= $1,563

We can see by this chart the power that leverage has in the total return potential on a portfolio. It is for this reason that I recommend a strong understanding of the options market and judicious use of options trading to enhance overall profitability.

Covered Calls

In this chapter we will learn about the exciting strategy of writing covered calls. Don't be concerned if you are not immediately familiar with what that term means, we will cover what you need to know to successfully employ this strategy as we move along in this chapter. This strategy deals with the process of generating a monthly income from a portfolio of stocks by selling options on those stocks. Income is generated by the option premium you receive when you sell the option. This strategy is the opposite side of the buying strategy discussed in the chapter "Options and You."

To put this strategy in perspective, let's first establish a basic fundamental truth about investing so that you can fully comprehend the process we are going to be discussing. Namely, that it is quite legal to sell something that you do not own in the securities markets of the United States. Now, that's not true throughout all the world markets, but here in the U. S., it's a very common occurrence among savvy investors. Selling something we do not own is done every day by thousands of people in the stock and options market. It does not mean that there are no rules or regulations, though. It means, simply, that there is a marketplace to sell securities that you do not own and that there are certain rules that must be followed in order that the process stays legally compliant and manageable. Once you know and understand those rules, this strategy is a snap, and a very exciting, convenient and profitable one at that.

What this strategy entails, in essence, is giving someone else the opportunity to buy your stock from you at a higher price than what you paid for it. This is accomplished by "selling" options to them to purchase your stock. The process of selling options that you DO NOT own, on stock that you DO own, is referred to as "writing." Writing is, simply, selling an option that you do not currently own. (If we did own it, we would plainly be selling it; not writing it.) As we discussed earlier in the book, a call option represents the right to buy a stock at a specific price for a certain period of time. When you sell a call option, you are giving someone else the right to buy your stock from you at the price that you agreed to sell it; the option strike price. By choosing a strike price above the price you paid for your stock, you are giving someone the right to buy your stock from you at a profit. It's really that simple.

As we said earlier, when you write an option, you give someone the right to purchase your stock. When you give them this right, you create an obligation for yourself by being required to hold on to the stock, and to deliver it for sale, should the buyer of the option want to purchase it. If you own the underlying stock on which you sold the option, as indicated above, your obligation to deliver the stock is "covered." Now, it is this process of purchasing stock and writing options on those stocks that we refer to as "writing covered calls." The "calls" refer, of course, to the type of options that we are writing; call options, as opposed to put options. Some stockbrokers also refer to this strategy as a "buy-write." Please know that it is exactly the same process; buying the stock and then writing the covered call, and the terms designate the same strategy.

The reason that we write these options is to generate an income. When we sell something, we get paid for it and when we sell an option, we get paid for it, too. Therefore, when we sell someone else the right to buy our stocks from us, they pay us a fee, called an option "premium," for that right. (They must, however, decide to buy the stock by the option expiration date, the third Friday of the month.) I, occasionally, use a metaphor at my seminars to further explain this strategy, that compares stocks to real estate, which seems to help people better understand covered call writing. For instance, let's say that you bought an apartment building as an investment hoping that it increased in value over the years that you intend to hold it. If the building does increase in value, say in five years, that's great. How would you generate an income from that investment, though, to pay maintenance bills, utilities, real estate taxes, etc.? The answer would be to rent out the apartment units to generate a monthly income to cover the expenses of owning the apartment building. So, think of the process of writing covered calls on your stocks as monthly rental income from your apartment building. Owning a portfolio of growth stocks is great. However, unless you sell some of those stocks on a monthly basis, virtually no income is generated from the portfolio. By writing covered calls on your portfolio, it's possible to generate a monthly income while you are waiting for your portfolio to increase in price. And, if your stocks are sold, (when the buyer exercises the options you wrote) you end up selling your stocks at a higher price than what you paid for them. At a nice profit! This is the essence of writing covered calls.

Now, by this time, you may have several questions in your mind as to how this strategy really works. Your first question may be something like "whom do I sell my options to" or, "Who would buy my stock for more than I paid for it," or something of that nature. Believe me, you will not have any trouble executing this strategy. There are hundreds of thousands of investors every month that use this strategy to supplement their income. I use it, too, on occasion for income and to offset downside risk in my portfolio. In answer to your first question, though, about who purchases the options that you want to sell, there is a marketplace called an exchange where all of the transactions take place. The exchange matches buyers and sellers to execute orders. That's what an exchange does. There are plenty of buyers out there for your options and it's your stockbroker's responsibility to place the order for you so that your order will be executed. It's that simple. As to who buys your stock, we never know the individual person or entity, and we do not care. We only know that if your stock rises substantially above the option strike price, that someone will buy it giving you a nice profit. How nice it feels when that happens.

Let's now use an actual example of a covered call write to illustrate this strategy. Let's say you owned 1,000 shares of a stock, we will call ABCD, that you purchased for about $18 per share. The stock does not pay a dividend and when you purchased the stock six months ago, you felt that it had prospects of rising to about $25. Since then, though, it has done virtually nothing and you would be happy to sell it for just about any price above what you paid for it. At this point, you may want to consider writing a covered call on the stock to generate some income and to offset the fact that the stock has done nothing for you for six months. Additionally, the prospects for the future do not appear as rosy as they did when you bought the stock in the first place. So, you call your stockbroker to get a market quote on the available options on this stock, and to see what income the prices may bring on a sale. As the stock is currently at $18, you know that there are options trading at strike prices of $17.50, $20 and $22.50. You, therefore, ask your broker for the quotes on these options expiring this month (March). The following is a list of the market quotes that you receive:

ABCD March $17.50 calls 1 x 1 3/8
*ABCD March $ 20 calls 1/2 x 3/4
ABCD March $ 22.50 calls 1/16 x 1/4

After examining the market quotes above, you quickly dismiss the March $22.50 calls because they would bring in only $62.50 in total income (1/16 times 10 contracts). Also, the March $17.50 calls would require you to sell the stock for less than it is currently selling for and even less than what you paid for it. That leaves the March $20 calls, then. In examining them, you find that you could gain $500 by selling the rights to purchase your stock for $20 per share (see asterisk). You could, in fact, write ten (10) contracts of the March $20 calls at a bid price of $1/2 dollar each (e.g., $1/2 times 10 contracts or one thousand shares) for a total price of $500. By doing this, you would generate an immediate income and lock in a potential capital gain of $2 per share if the stock rose above $20. Since you paid $18 for the stock (or $18,000 on 1,000 shares), by generating an income of $500 you have created an investment yield of 2.7% ($500 divided by $18,000). If you had done that each and every month the last six months that you owned the stock, you could conceivably have generated a 16.6% return so far this year on your investments. Even if the stock does not rise in price, 16.6% is not a bad return on your investment. But, that's only half the story. If the stock does rise in price, to say $21.50 during the lifetime of your option, the purchaser of the option will exercise his right to buy your stock for $20. When he does this, you will have locked in a capital gain of $2 per share, or $2,000 total. This $2,000, when added to the $500 you previously received, gives you a total income of $2,500. This now represents a powerful 13.9% return for the month! Even though you had to sell the stock at less than full market value, due to writing the options, your return is still very respectable. As you can see, though, you must be willing to limit the potential growth in a stocks' price if you are going to use this strategy. The best part now, however, is that you know that you can continue to use this strategy every month to produce notable results.

Let's take another example. Let's say that you are thinking of the best way to invest $10,000 to maximize your income and to allow for some growth in your stock portfolio, too. You discuss this idea with your stockbroker and he suggests that you purchase XYZA stock that is selling at about $9 per share. He tells you that XYZA is a growing company and the stock has been as high as $15 this year and as low as $7. XYZA has options trading on its' stock and your broker gives you the current option prices that are as follows:

XYZA March $10 calls   1 x 1 3/8
XYZA March $12.50 calls   1/2 x 3/4

Now, before you purchase the stock there are several things that you should know about the company as we have discussed in other chapters. However, in this case, let's assume that XYZA meets all of your investment criteria as well as your risk tolerance. You are now ready to invest your money if you can get a good return on your investment. Let's assume, like before, that you would be willing to purchase 1,000 shares of stock and that you would pay $9 per share, or $9,000. Purchasing 1,000 shares of XYZA stock would allow you to write ten contracts of the $10 or $12.50 calls to get a return on your investment. Let's examine which choice gives you the best total return.

By writing the XYZA March $10 calls, your option premium income would be $1,000 (e.g., ten (10) contracts times the $1 bid price of the option, equals $1,000). The current yield on your investment would then be computed by taking the $1,000 and dividing it by your investment amount of $9,000. ($1,000/$9000) That equals 11.1% current yield on your investment. If the stock rises above $10 per share and is exercised, you will have a capital gain. The capital gain is computed by subtracting the price you paid for the stock ($9) from the strike price of the option that you wrote ($10). Your capital gain, therefore, would be an additional $1,000. Add that to the original $1,000 option premium income, and you find this transaction has the potential to provide a $2,000 profit. This profit, then, equates to a 22.2% total return potential. Before making your decision, however, we have to examine the opportunities presented by the $12.50 strike price option.

Writing the March $12.50 calls would bring an income of $500 when sold at the bid price of $1/2; a current return of 5.5%. The potential for capital gains, though, would be far greater. The potential capital gain would be $3.50 per share, or a total of $3,500 (the difference between the $9 stock and the $12.50 option, is $3.50). That sum, when combined with the option premium income of $500, would give you a total profit potential on the transaction of $4,000, or a possible total return of 44.4%.

So, now it is up to you to decide which option contract to write. There really is no right or wrong answer. Only what you feel is right for you. Are you willing to take a reasonable return of 11.1% with an opportunity to make 22.2%, or do you wish to take only a 5.5% return for the chance to make a whopping 44.4%? Or, perhaps, you wish to take a combination of both opportunities. The choices are yours. However, you must examine all of your possibilities before making a final decision. I always "run the numbers" (as we did above) before I make a decision on which option to write. I even run the numbers before I buy the stock, itself. I look to see which stock gives me the highest yield and the best opportunity for profit. You should, too. By examining your choices in this way you will always come up with the investment solution that's right for you.

There are a few guidelines that I would like you to consider when you are examining potential stocks to purchase for covered call writing that may come in handy. First, that the stock should be of good quality and commensurate with your risk tolerance and investment objectives. Second, that there has been substantial price movement (volatility) in the stock and that it has not languished at a particular price level for a long period of time. Lastly, the stocks' price should be between $8 and $25 per share. Stocks at lower prices allow for better diversification of your portfolio. Since you can only lose what you invest, lower priced stocks in a well-diversified portfolio also tend to reduce your exposure to large losses. Additionally, you have more profit opportunities and investment choices with lower priced stocks because the option strike prices are in increments of only $2.50. These are only a sampling of ideas to follow, I'm sure that you will establish additional rules for yourself as you continue to employ this strategy successfully over time.

Index Options

Index options are interesting investment vehicles for the more experienced investor who wishes to hedge an existing portfolio of stocks or take a speculative position in trading the stock market. Let's first discuss what an index option is and then look at an example of how they are used, and finally, how you can apply them profitably to your own investment strategies.

THE INDEX

An index, itself, is a way of measuring, or evaluating, a group of stocks based on their aggregate price. The index is a hypothetical value of the total stock prices, which are initially assigned an arbitrary representative value. (It's like asking someone how they feel on a scale of 1 to 10. They do not really feel like a number, but it is representative of how they feel based on 10 being great.) If we were to start our own stock index today using a portfolio of 10 different stocks, we might assign the index an initial value of 100.00

based on the closing prices of those 10 stocks. As those prices change and go up and down, the index will correspondingly be increased or decreased according to that price change. Some stocks in the index may be weighted greater than others because the increase or decrease in their price may have more of a dramatic effect on the overall change in stock market direction. Basically, that's what an index is in a nutshell.

There are three primary stock indexes that are traded on the exchange and each represents a different value index. The three primary indexes are: the Standard and Poor's 500 Index (SPX) which represents 500 stocks, the Standard and Poor's 100 Index (OEX) representing 100 stocks, and the Major Market Index (XMI) which includes 20 stocks.

The SPX (usually referred to as the S&P 500) includes 500 stocks which trade on both the New York Stock Exchange (NYSE) and on NASDAQ. It's like the "Fortune 500" of companies, and is the broadest representation of overall stock market performance and, perhaps, the most popular of the indexes to watch. The S&P 100, or the OEX as it's usually called, represents 100 stocks, all of which trade on the NYSE, and includes the 30 stocks in the Dow Jones Industrial Average (DJIA), as well. The Major Market Index, called the XMI, represents the 20 highest capitalized and widely recognized stocks listed on the NYSE. It currently comprises 19 of the 30 stocks in the DJIA; stocks like IBM, Merck, GE, Proctor & Gamble, Coke, AT&T and others, are included.

Now, each of these indexes has options trading, both puts and calls, just as stocks do. The options have different strike prices and are quoted and traded based on changes in the index value, again, just as stock options trade on the price changes of their respective stocks. There are option strike prices usually set at 5 point increments of the index value and generally extend very deep in-the-money, as well as far out-of-the-money. To use an example of options strike prices, let's look at where the OEX index stands now. The price of the OEX index is currently at 625.32. (It is sometimes helpful to look at an index's value like dollars and cents. There is a direct relationship in stock indexes as you will see later, so think of the index as if it were $625.32.) There are options trading on this index with strike prices of 600, 605, 610, 620, 625, 630, 635, etc. As you can see, the strike prices are in increments of $5. New strike prices are added as needed (as demand indicates), i.e., whenever the index touches an existing strike price at the upper or lower end of the scale. As in stock options, each 1-point move in the index represents $100, and the settlement of purchases and sales will occur the next business day. Trading in the index options begins at 9:30 AM Eastern Time and extends until 4:15 PM. The options expire at the same time equity options do, and the last opportunity to trade them is the third Friday of the expiration month.

When getting a market quote on an index option, one would select the trading month (current month or following month) and the option strike price; then ask the broker for the quote. Example: "Please give me a quote on the OEX March 630 call options." The broker will respond with a market quote just as he would if he were quoting stock options. "The OEX March 630's are currently quoted at 4 1/4 by 4 3/4" is the broker's reply, for example. Index options trading is fairly easy and any broker should be able to assist you in placing your order.

USES

Index options are used in two primary ways: for outright speculation and for hedging an existing portfolio. As you might imagine, it's the speculation that fortunes are to be made quickly that entices everyone to trade the indexes. The value of the indexes' changes dramatically during the average trading day and it is not unusual for the value of an index option to double at some point from it's daily low. For the amateur, it is fairly unpredictable, though, and is little more than an outright gamble on the direction of the market. More poor persons than rich ones have been made from such activities in the past. However, if a person estimates correctly, there is substantial reward for the endeavor; the reverse is also true if a person estimates incorrectly.

Should we decide to speculate in index options, there are many choices (strike prices) available. The OEX index, mentioned earlier, was at 625.32, and there are options available at various strike prices. Each strike price will have a different market price according to its' demand and its' proximity (in or out of-the-money) to the current value of the actual index. With the index at 625.32, we might receive the following quotes from our broker when we inquired during the trading day:

OEX Mar 625 call 21 1/2 x 22 3/4, put 20 7/8 x 21 3/4
OEX Mar 630 call 18 5/8 x 19 1/2, put 18 x 19 1/8
OEX Mar 635 call 15 7/8 x 16 3/8, put 15 1/2 x 16 1/8
OEX Mar 640 call 12 3/4 x 13 1/8, put 12 x 12 3/4
OEX Mar 645 call 8 3/4 x 9 5/8, put 8 1/8 x 8 7/8

After getting these quotes, we would need to decide which option represented our best short-term opportunity for profit. And, since these options are very expensive, we cannot afford to be wrong for long. Most of these options would cost us well over $1,000.00 or more. Although it is probable that they will change price rapidly throughout the day, it's a large investment to make in one option contract. Purchasing several contracts could be devastating should the market react opposite to our assumptions. However, the purchase of several contracts could make tens of thousands of dollars if the market reacts as we anticipated. We will cover more about choosing option contracts a little later in this chapter.

Looking beyond the speculation on major market moves, though, there is a useful tool for hedging the potential decline of a stock portfolio available to us through the efficient use of index options. As I mentioned earlier, there are both, call and put options available on the indexes, and put options give us a high degree of leverage and portfolio protection in declining markets. Put options, as you know, become more valuable as the index declines. And, since the index represents the overall price movements of the stock market, the index will obviously decline in value along with stock prices overall. By purchasing put options on one of the indexes we can effectively hedge much of the price decline in a stock portfolio.

Which index's option to purchase is the next question that we will need to confront. (I usually trade the OEX options because they have great liquidity and many institutions trade these options, too. There are the other indexes, as well, of course, and they can be just as effective for hedging, but I have many years experience trading the OEX, which is why I usually trade that one. Like most people, I feel more comfortable investing in something I am familiar with.) You may have an index that is a particular favorite, as I do. The important thing to remember is to choose an index that best represents the make-up of your stock portfolio. Selection of a broad based index, or one more narrow in scope, should be commensurate with your overall investment objectives and the type of stocks that you own. After selecting the index, let's use what we have learned so far to determine how index options can best be applied to our advantage.

THE STRATEGIES

I mentioned earlier that there was a relationship between the value of an index and its' measurement in terms of dollars and cents. Let's examine that relationship so that we can determine the number of contracts that are necessary to effectively hedge our portfolio. Take, for example, the OEX index that was listed earlier at a value of 625.32. This value actually represents a selected stock portfolio worth $62,532.00. Theoretically, this portfolio could be hedged, then, through the purchase of one (1) put option contract since each contract would represent an index having the same dollar value. As the value of that $62,532 portfolio declines, the put options would, again theoretically, increase in value by the same amount that the portfolio declined. Therefore, as the theory holds, if we had a large portfolio worth, let's say, $625,320 we would need to purchase ten (10) options contracts to effectively hedge that size portfolio, for example. I used the term "theoretically" because in actual practice the forces of the market play a very large role in the price movements of index options. In practice, the absolute stock price declines tend to be greater than the actual increases in the price of the put options. (Call options on the index, though, tend to gain price increases more rapidly in upward markets that the put options do in downward markets.) In most market declines, the increase in option premiums of at-the-money put options are equal to roughly 60% of the actual decline in the price of the stocks. In a $62,532 portfolio, we would have to purchase two (2) at-the-money options at the cost of over $4,000 just to hedge against the decline in this manner. This is not a reasonable sum of money to spend each month for portfolio protection. How then, might we accomplish what we set out to accomplish without spending such an unreasonable amount of money?

I have found that the best way to reasonably hedge against a portfolio decline without paying excessive portfolio "insurance" premiums is to buy a current month put option five (5) strike prices out-of-the-money. The purchase price of that option is nearly always less than one-half of what an at-the-money put option would cost, and it usually moves the equivalent of 55% as much as the at-the-money put option would. Therefore, if we were so inclined, we could actually buy twice as many out-of-the-money put options for less than the price of the at-the-money options and get more than 110% of the protection. However, no matter which index option we purchase it's possible to hedge only about 60% of our portfolio decline, dollar for dollar, and be cost effective. So the purchase of one option, five strike prices out-of-the-money makes the most sense in the majority of cases. Remember that hedging is really insuring against a potential loss, and that most of us are willing to spend just so much money to hedge against a loss. You may wish to liken the payment of option premiums to those of insurance premiums, and refer to the remaining portion of a loss as that which is uninsured, or the "deductible" portion of a loss that the policy does not cover.

That's essentially the case here. The cost of complete and total coverage is greater than the potential loss in many cases, but puts can be used as a reasonable hedge, nonetheless.

Let's revisit, for now, how we might go about choosing the purchase of an index option contract to maximize our investment returns if we are speculating on price movements in the stock market. Referring to the previous pages listing the options' prices of the OEX index, please take a look at the call options prices for a moment. Let's assume that we have a strong feeling, based on our research, that the stock market is going to rise 10% over the next 30 days. The OEX index currently stands at the 625.32 level and, as we have indicated before, a 10% increase in the overall market would probably increase the index by about 10%, as well. That move, then, could propel the level of the OEX to nearly 688.00 (up 10%). With that index value increase, the index call options would have moved significantly higher, as well. Let's see how much we might have made if we had invested in the call options and which call option series might have been the best one to buy. (Prices are before and after the stock market rise.)

	Before	After
OEX Mar 625 call	21 1/2 x 22 3/4,	65 x 67
OEX Mar 630 call	18 5/8 x 19 1/2,	60 1/4 x 62 1/4
OEX Mar 635 call	15 7/8 x 16 3/8,	55 5/8 x 57 5/8
OEX Mar 640 call	12 3/4 x 13 1/2,	52 x 54
OEX Mar 645 call	8 3/4 x 9 5/8,	47 1/2 x 49 1/2

If we had purchased the March 625 call, which would have been an at-the-money option at the time of our proposed purchase, we would have paid approximately $2,275 when buying on the offer (ask) side of the market. That option would have then risen to approximately $6,500 in the ensuing market rise, and we would be able to sell it for that price when selling on the bid side of the market. The increase, then, in our investment would be a total of approximately $4,225 ($6,500 less $2,275, excluding commission). Our investment return would then be a robust 185%. Not bad for a few days work. However, if we had purchased an out-of-the money option say, the 645 call, our investment return would have been significantly better.

The OEX March 635 call would cost us $962.50; the equivalent of 9 5/8 times one contract (on the offer side of the market). We could sell that call now at the bid price of $4,750, or a profit of $3,787.50. That would provide an investment return in excess of 390% ($3,787.50 divided by $962.50). Significantly better than what we would have gotten if we had purchased an at-the-money call option for a great deal more money. Remember, when purchasing options, you can only lose the amount of money that you invest, so it is better to invest a little, rather than a lot. Also, out-of-the-money options will nearly always provide a better percentage investment return than at-the-money or in-the-money options. The same holds true for equity options, as well.

When speculating in index options, I usually buy an option 4 or 5 strike prices out-of-the-money to maximize my returns and reduce my investment risk. That's the name of the game in options. If you desire to speculate in index options, the use of this strategy can be both fun and profitable when the market moves your way.

Straddles and Strangles

One of the best strategies available to make money, involves the simultaneous purchase of a call and a put on the same stock at the same strike price. This is called a "Straddle". The assumption is that no matter which way the stock moves, we will participate in that movement in a profitable manner. If the stock shows strong growth (upside movement) we would participate on the call side of the straddle. Conversely, should the stock show weakness, we would have a put that would increase in value as the stock declined.

At first glance, it may seem that this strategy is foolproof. Well, in the stock market, nothing is quite that simple. There are some necessary guidelines that must be followed in order that the transaction has a chance of being profitable and that you don't get into a stock that has little, if any, chance of making you any money. Let's look at some of the criteria for stock selection and then we'll review what techniques work best using this strategy.

First and foremost, it is important that the stock we select to purchase has sufficient volatility to move in either direction in a profitable manner. It is true that by using this strategy we can profit in either direction the stock moves, but the stock must move. If it stays at the price same price it was when the transaction was initiated without some movement, we will nearly always lose on the trade. Therefore, we want volatility (up and down movement) in the stock. Determining volatility is easy if we have the right tools. I use a charting service that provides daily price movement of the stock. I look for stocks that have chart "patterns" that tell me how much a stock has moved, in terms of price, over a fairly short period of time (volatility). There are many stocks that exhibit patterns with significant enough volatility to be profitable using this strategy. All one has to do is look through a series of charts to find the right stock. Once a stock is found that looks like it could be a good trade, that stock can be kept in our arsenal to be played over and over again until it no longer meets the volatility criteria. Many times the same stock can be played for years, or at least many months, before it loses its volatility. We will keep an eye on the chart as we trade, though, for signs of reduced trading activity and volatility. We will know as time goes on if this stock is one that we will want to continually play, just by watching its activity while we are still trading it. (Show chart of a stock with volatility.)

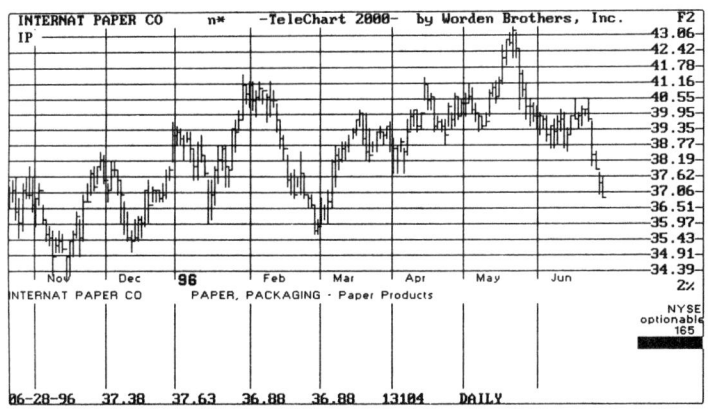

How to Invest Your Way to Wealth

Knowing that volatility is the first thing we need, what comes next? The answer to that is to determine the price that we will pay for the combined options. If we were to watch a particular stock and find that it had jumped up dramatically due to a recent news item (earnings outlook, perhaps) we probably couldn't be sure if it was going to continue to go up or come back to prior trading levels. If the stock has just jumped 10 points in the last 5 trading days, we could never be sure if it was going to continue to increase, or if it was going to succumb to profit taking and decline to previous prices. We may at this point then, decide to do our straddle. We would buy a put and a call option at the same strike price with the same expiration. The key is not to spend too much money, in other words, not to spend more than a certain percentage of what the expected price movement in the stock would be. If we think that the stock is going to move up another 5 points or that it could go down 5 points, that's a 10 point swing. But if we pay too much for the combined options, we may never be able to profit even if the stock does what we want and expect it to do. So, the rule of thumb in this transaction will be that we never want to spend more than 50% of the expected movement of the stock for both our options combined. This means that if we think the stock could go up 10 points or down 10 points we don't want to spend more than $5.00 for both, the put and the call. Now, we might think, "That's a lot of money to spend on an option," but remember, we already determined that this stock was volatile and would move in one direction or the other and that it would, definitely not, stay at this price level. So, if XYZ stock were at, let's say, $75.00 per share we would be buying the XYZ $75 puts and the XYZ $75 calls for a combined "Premium" (option cost) of no more than $5.00. If XYZ continues to move up, the calls will be worth more than the amount of money we would lose on the puts. If the stock goes down dramatically, the puts will be worth more than the amount that is lost on the calls. Using the above example, let's say that XYZ moved from $75.00 per share to $80.00 within three trading days of our purchasing the straddle. The $75.00 calls would be worth, probably $6 to $7. The $75.00 puts would be worth, perhaps, $1. Combined value is $7 to $8; about a 40% to 60% gain on our investment in three days. Not too bad. If we adhere to the rules of not paying more than 50% of the expected movement for the combined options, we should have many, many happy and profitable trading days.

There is another way to play this same strategy, though, and involves another technique that I like a little better because it requires less capital to execute. This technique, although it is a type of straddle, is called a "Strangle". A strangle involves "surrounding" the stock, with a purchase of both a put and a call, but at different strike prices. If XYZ stock was at $73.00 per share, a strangle could be established with the purchase of an XYZ $75 call, and an XYZ $70 put. This surrounds the stocks' current price and will again allow for a profitable trade if the stock moves dramatically in one direction or the other. The rule of thumb for this technique states that we should not spend more than 30% of the expected price movement for the purchase of both the put and call. Therefore, we are required to put up less money per transaction allowing us to purchase more contracts (use more leverage) than with a conventional straddle. We MUST be sure that the stock will move, however. If the stock stays at the current level, we will lose on both sides of the transaction. Although the strangle offers greater leverage, it also has greater risk if the stock stagnates at its current price.

Option Spreads

Let us now take a look at how another option strategy can be used profitably with a technique involving option "Spreads."

Definition

A spread is a dual option strategy that involves the purchase and sale of two different strike prices of calls or puts on the same underlying stock. The investor executing a spread will hope that the underlying stock will move in the preferred direction so that he may close out his transaction profitably with limited risk. A spread involves the purchase of an option with a particular strike price, and the sale of an option (of the same class) with a different strike price.

A call spread involves the purchase of a call option with a strike price typically lower than the strike price of the call that is sold. (example buy 10 AT&T June $60 calls and write 10 AT&T June $65 calls). The investor will profit if AT&T stays above the $60 price by an amount greater than his net cost of the transaction. (This is called a "Covered" transaction because the investor has the right to buy the stock at a lower price ($60) should he be exercised on the $65 call.)

(AT&T stock price $61)

Buy 10 AT&T June 60 Calls @ 2 3/4 =	$2,750
Sell 10 AT&T June 65 Calls @ 7/8 =	- $875
Net Cost	$1,875

In the above example the investors net cost of the transaction is $1,875 (or 1 7/8 if quoted as a fraction). If AT&T moves above the investors net cost $61 7/8, the transaction is profitable. If AT&T should move above $65, the maximum amount the investor can make is the difference between the two strike prices of the options. Therefore, if AT&T moved above $65 by June, the investor would close out his transaction and would theoretically receive $5,000 (the difference between the two strike prices). His profit would be the difference between $5,000 and the amount that he paid ($1,875), or $3,125. I use the word "theoretically" because the mathematical difference is the $5 between the strike prices. In actuality, the differential is closer to 4 3/4, with the remainder being the spread that the market maker is going to take relative to closing out the investors' transaction.

An option spread can be developed at different time intervals or it can be accomplished simultaneously with the purchase and sale of the options occurring at once. When executed simultaneously, the investor would give his broker an order using the term "Net Debit". This means that the purchase and sale of the options contracts will result in a net cost to the investor not to exceed the net debit amount. Using the above example, the investor would place the order using a net debit of 1 7/8. The price of both option contracts may continue to change rapidly in a fast moving market but the investor will not execute his traded unless he pays the equivalent of 1 7/8, or less.

A spread may be developed individually, as well, with an investor purchasing a particular option contract as an initial or "Opening" transaction. As the underlying stock begins to move in the desired direction, the investor may be willing to limit his profit potential (and his risk) by "Writing" (selling) another option contract, thereby bringing money into his account and reducing the cost basis of his investment in the original contract purchased.

Uses

Spreads can be used for several reasons particularly when an investor wants to reduce his cost of an option transaction and is also willing to limit his profit potential (again, to a maximum of the difference between the two strike prices).

Typically, call spreads are the most popular, but put spreads can work well in a declining market, too. In a put spread, the investor will purchase an option having a higher strike price than a put that he sells. This also is considered a covered transaction. As the stock declines, the puts become more valuable. When the stock declines to a point where both options are "In-the-money" or the far option contract is "At-the-money," the investor will liquidate the position, which has, again, reached the maximum potential profit level. This transaction, too, can be executed individually or as a unit. Generally speaking, spreads liquidated as a unit will usually result in better execution prices for the investor. I would recommend that spreads be liquidated together to maximize price and yield potential. When liquidating, the order given to the broker would be for a "Net Credit," rather than a net debit amount and would be executed if the price reaches that net credit level or higher.

Spreads can also be used in the same manner as are "Covered Calls." We think of writing covered calls for income purposes and for portfolio hedges. They can also be used to generate income on higher priced stocks rather than buying the stock itself. Even if one were to purchase a high-priced stock on margin, it would probably require more investment capital than a well planned spread.

Let's look at the following example to illustrate this point. If an investor were to purchase 1,000 shares of Microsoft stock with the stock being around $130/share, he would need to have at least $65,000 in cash to execute the trade, even on a margin basis. Since his goal is to make money if Microsoft stock increases, he may be able to accomplish the same task by purchasing 10 contracts of the Microsoft $115 calls (which would be deep in-the-money) for about $20, and writing the Microsoft $140 calls for about $6. The net cost would then be approximately $14,000, rather than $65,000. If Microsoft stock were to climb to $140/share or higher, the spread can then be liquidated at a net credit of $25,000. This trade, then, would result in a net profit of $11,000, or a cash-on-cash return of approximately 78%. This strategy would also require much less investment capital than the outright purchase of the stock.

Calendar Spreads

A calendar spread is one where the underlying purchased option contract has a maturity longer than that of the contract that is written. It is not unusual for this strategy to be employed when option contracts are purchased on higher priced stocks, (as in the Microsoft example above). On many occasions an investor may purchase a long-term call thinking the price may rise over time, yet write a short-term call thinking that the stock may stay in a lower range in the near term. Calendar spreads can also be used very effectively with "L.E.A.P.S." as an income producer, as well as long-term equity appreciation investments.

Rules of Thumb

There are a few guidelines to remember when executing spread transactions that will help us maximize our profit potential and limit possible losses. The rules include:

A) Limit any net debit amount to no more than 50% of the difference between strike prices. (If the strike prices are five points apart, we should not pay more than two and one-half as a net debit, maximum.)

B) In most spread transactions the most that we can usually make is twice our investment. We should not get too greedy! If we get only a 50% or 75% return let's be happy and get out.

C) We should invest only in option contracts of volatile stocks.

D) We should use limit orders when liquidating our spread transactions.

E) We should liquidate our spread as a
unit, not separately, to get the best
execution prices.

The Psychology of Investing

One of the most difficult areas of effective portfolio management to teach is the "psychology of investing" for profit. Everyone is willing to take a profit. Few, are willing to take a loss on their investments, and will even tend to hold losing positions for years waiting for the prices to return to profitable levels before shedding the investments from their portfolio.

There are three main areas that we will discuss in this book to assist the reader in identifying potential short-comings to profitable portfolio management. Remember, I'm talking portfolio management. It doesn't matter how big your portfolio is, necessarily; it could be $5,000 or $500,000. The principles remain the same. The three areas of discussion include: a) pitfalls to watch out for, b) when to take profits, c) when to take losses. The last one may seem to be a forbidden subject to some, but there is not a person alive who has been trading longer than 3 months who hasn't had a loss in something.

PITFALLS. Our human psyche is so fragile at times that most of us refuse to recognize the symptoms of poor judgment. When we make a decision we make a decision. That's it! Good, bad or indifferent, we've made a decision and we're going to stick to it. Sometimes this refusal to admit mistakes can be our downfall.

Over centuries there have been dozens of examples of famous, successful men who have been victimized by their own inability to admit error. Call it ego, vanity, over-confidence or whatever. It is purely and simply a mistake to be so obstinate. None of us are infallible (although many of us think we are) and we all make decisions that we have regretted from time to time. How do we keep from making them and how do we correct them when we do, is the question.

I'm going to use the example of what can happen in a stock portfolio to illustrate my point in this case. Let's say that we have purchased five different stocks at five different times over the last several months and that our portfolio is now fully invested. (If we started with $10,000 in cash, we purchased $10,000 worth of stocks). News comes out regarding a stock that we have been watching for quite some time for an opportunity to buy. We feel the timing is right, but we don't have any "buying power" to purchase the stock when we want to. We decide that it may now be a good time to sell some of our existing portfolio of stocks so that we can buy into this new opportunity. Looking at our portfolio and getting current quote information, we determine that the five stocks have the following profits and losses:

Stock A- $ 1,200 profit   **Stock D** - $ 1,600 loss
Stock B - $ 900 loss   **Stock E** - $ 600 profit
Stock C - $ 2,300 profit

Knowing that we will need to sell at least two of our existing stocks to make our new purchase we examine the above table. If we are like most people, our first thought is that Stock A, C or E might be the best candidates to sell to provide for this new purchase. After all, we do have a profit in these stocks and even though they have been good investments, it may be time to take the profits and run. Of course, we would never even dream of selling Stocks B or D because, after all, we have a loss in these stocks. It would be unthinkable to imagine taking a loss. These stocks will surely come back to the levels that we paid for them, and then, and only then, would we think about selling them. We, therefore; put in an order to sell Stocks A and C because those represent the largest profits in our portfolio. It is OK to take profits, never losses, we think. So, as time goes by, we now have just three stocks in our portfolio. The new stock we purchased (we'll call Stock F) is about the same price that we paid for it, but the other two have continued their decline. Stock B now is worth $1,200 less than what we paid for it and Stock D is worth $1,900 less. Slowly our overall profits are being eroded because of our insistence of holding on to our losers. After several weeks, Stock F has performed well showing a nice gain of some $600. Stocks B and D, however, have continued their slide and now are worth a combined $4,000 less than what we paid for them. Actually , we are now in a position where our overall portfolio is only slightly ahead of the amount that we started investing with. We have been right on our stock selection in 4 out of 6 cases, yet our portfolio is only slightly ahead, and after income taxes on the gains, we have an actual loss in terms of dollars.

It would have been far more sensible for us to have taken our losses in the stocks that weren't performing well for us so that we could take a position in Stock F. We would have kept our "winners" and sold our "losers", thus creating a tax loss benefit and still being able to buy Stock F. We would then have a portfolio of four stocks all of which would be "winners". It sometimes pays very handsomely to accept the small losses and get into something else. Keeping our winners and selling our losers has made more rich men than poor. It is an investment strategy used most effectively by Warren Buffet, whom I consider to be the premier securities investor of our time. It is also the best way to keep our tax liability as low as possible. Over the long run, we'll benefit nicely from this strategy if we refuse to allow our ego to get in the way of making intelligent business decisions. Remember, the stock we bought has no idea what we paid for it. It may never get back to the level that we paid. If we made a bad decision, get rid of it. Sometimes we have to take a step back in order to take two steps forward. This is one such example.

WHEN TO TAKE PROFITS - I like to think about taking profits when I've made more money than I can ever spend. I like to think about this; it hasn't happened yet, but it's fun just to imagine. For the reader, though, I would advise on taking profits when situations in the stock have changed that indicate the stock is no longer a bargain at the present price level. What I mean is, simply, that when a stock climbs significantly from the price we paid for it, we have to ask ourselves if we would still want to buy it at these levels. If the answer is yes, then hold onto it. If the answer is otherwise, it could be time to sell.

When someone purchases a stock, they probably have in mind a pre-conceived price level at which they would be willing to sell that stock. It may be significantly more than what was paid for the stock, or it could be only modestly more. Whenever the stock reaches that sell point, the investor must watch it closely to see if it is going to continue to rise, or if it will decline due to selling pressure from others. I like to use "sell-stop" orders when my stocks reach the levels that I am looking to achieve. Sell-stop orders are placed at prices below the current price of the stock so that if a stock begins to drop back, eroding profits, the stock will be sold to protect those profits. If the stock continues to rise, then one would continue to participate in those profits and would increase the price of the sell-stop order to protect those additional profits, as well. Deciding when to take a profit can be nearly as difficult for some of us as taking a loss on occasion; therefore, we have to be ever mindful of the future growth prospects for our stocks at every price level. Stocks that go up tend to keep going up. Stocks that decline tend to do the same. We must keep an open mind when evaluating the current prospects for our investments by asking ourselves if we would buy the stock at this new price level. If the answer is no, it could well be time to sell.

WHEN TO TAKE A LOSS - Let me make one thing "perfectly clear". I never like to take losses. It doesn't mean that I don't, though. Taking a loss is always a psychological blow to the ego. But there is an old saying on Wall Street that your "first loss is your best loss". I never could figure out how any loss would be a best loss until it happened to me one day in what turned out to be a textbook example. Being able to decide quickly when to take a loss is important, as we will soon see. Like most people, though, I prefer to think of taking profits, and try not to practice the art of being a good loser. Learning from my experiences, though, may be helpful to the reader trying to decide whether or not to take a loss. If not, at least it will be entertaining.

I wanted to purchase call options on IBM stock several years ago and made the mistake of purchasing put options instead. (Don't ask how; it just happened.) When I realized my mistake only a few minutes later, I had a paper loss of $2,700. "Unbelievable," I thought. "How could this happen to me?". Well, sometimes mistakes are made. Pure and simple. We are all human and we are all prone to mistakes at times. I surely didn't want to take a $2,700 loss in a period of about one hour. But, after conferring with some of my colleagues, (I was really looking for sympathy more than information) it was determined that I should take the loss. Kicking and screaming, I decided that I would. It's a good thing, too! If I had waited until the end of the day as I had planned (hoping that the stock would come back) I would have lost $16,000. Now THAT would have been a real "kick in the shorts".

I learned first hand what they meant (whoever "they" is) when they said "Your first loss is your best loss". Sometimes the stock just never comes back. IBM did, though. It took about three years, but it finally came back to where I would have bought it had the trade been done properly. I learned a substantial lesson then and I would hope that the reader learn from me rather than from experience. (Experience is nearly always more painful.) If stocks aren't' working for us, we need to sell them. There are plenty of good opportunities out there for us rather than to sit with a portfolio of losers. I don't necessarily mean to sell the same day that we buy, as I was forced to do, only that if an investment isn't working for us, then it will probably eventually work against us. Get out of it and move on.

The Ten Commandments

--(of Investing)--

1) Diversify, diversify and then, diversify!
2) Buy on weakness -- Sell on strength.
3) Maximize profits and limit losses with stop orders.
4) Don't let your ego get in the way of good decisions!
5) Don't fall in "love" with your investments -- Learn to sell if necessary.
6) Don't get greedy!
7) Think short-term, "How much can I make this week?"
8) Do your "homework"-.Investigate and research.
9) If investment parameters change, get out!
10) Never, ever risk more than you can afford to lose.

Glossary of Terms

Call-   An option contract giving the option holder the right, but not the obligation, to buy the underlying company stock at a specific price for a certain period of time.

Class-   A group of options consisting of either puts or calls.

Contract-   The minimum trading unit for options. Each contract represents 100 shares of stock in the underlying company.

Covered-   An option term meaning that an option writer owns, or has the right to buy, the underlying stock of a particular company on which he has sold the right to purchase it to someone else.

Discount-   The rate that the Federal Reserve Board charges member banks for borrowing funds. An increase in the rate is an attempt to restrict the money supply to ward off inflationary pressures.

DJIA- The Dow Jones Industrial Average. It is a weighted index representing the underlying prices, or values, of the common stock of 30 (thirty) selected, large U.S. industrial companies.

Exercise- The right of the option holder to require an option writer to deliver the stock of the underlying company for purchase at the strike price.

Margin- Borrowing money from a brokerage firm or a bank for the purpose of purchasing securities which will act as collateral for the loan.

At-the-money- An option contract where the strike price is equal to the current price of the stock.

In-the-money- A call option contract where the strike price is below the current price of the underlying stock, or a put option contract where the strike price is above the current price of the underlying stock.

Out-of-the-money- A call option contract where the strike price is above the current price of the stock, or a put option contract where the strike price is below the current price of the stock.

Naked- An option term meaning that an option writer does not own, or have the prior right to buy, the underlying company stock although he has sold the right to purchase it from him to someone else.

Option- A contract representing 100 shares of stock that gives the holder the right, but not the obligation, to buy or sell 100 shares each option contract) of the underlying stock at a certain price (the strike price) for a specific period of time.

Put- An option which gives the holder the right, but not the obligation, to sell the underlying company stock at a specific price for a certain period of time.

Spread- The purchase of an option contract and sale of another option contract, of the same class, having two different strike prices.

Straddle- An option strategy involving the purchase of both a put and a call on the same stock with the same strike price and expiration.

Strangle- An option strategy involving the purchase of a put below the current price of the underlying stock and the purchase of a call above the current price, both having the same expiration.

Strike price- The price at which the holder of an option contract can exercise his right to buy or sell the underlying stock.

Write- An option term synonymous with the word "sell". The initial sale of an option contract can be either covered or naked depending upon the writers ownership of the underlying stock.

Zero Coupon Bond- A derivative debt security that pays no interest and sells at a deep discount to maturity (face) value.